Fulton's Footprints in FIJI

Fulton's Footprints in FIJI

ERIC B. HARE

Lives of great men all remind us
We can make our lives sublime,
And, departing, leave behind us
Footprints on the sands of time.
—HENRY WADSWORTH LONGFELLOW

Pacific Press Publishing Association
Boise, Idaho
Montemorelos, Nuevo Leon, Mexico
Oshawa, Ontario

Library of Congress Cataloging in Publication Data

Hare, Eric B.
   Fulton's footprints in Fiji.

   Originally published: Washington: Review and Herald Pub.
Association, 1969.
   Bibliography: p.
   1. Fulton, John Edwin, 1869-1945. 2. Missionaries—Fiji—
Biography. 3. Missionaries—United States—Biography. 4.
Seventh-Day Adventists—Missions—Fiji.
I. Title.
BV3680.F6F8   1985   266'.6732'0924 [B]   84-16515

ISBN 0-8163-0583-8

85 86 87 88 89 • 6 5 4 3 2 1

Foreword

In the natural turn of events, I fell heir to the file containing the carbon copies of the stories and articles that John Edwin Fulton wrote during his lifetime.

I have obtained much help in establishing the sequence of the experiences, and in gathering the human interest that rounds them out and makes them live, from the following persons:

Alice Cross, daughter of Ella Fulton, the younger sister of John Fulton.

Tavita Cole, son of John Cole, born in Fiji.

A. G. Stewart, one of Australia's great missionary heroes, who spent fourteen years in Fiji.

Eva Edwards, who was part of the Fulton family for some time and spent twenty-five years in Fiji.

Septimus Carr, another great Australian missionary, who gave twenty-three years to Fiji.

Enid and Len Wilkinson, who gave thirteen years to Fiji in educational and administrative work.

And Ray Wilkinson, a second-generation missionary who is still in Fiji.

But above all, I am indebted to John Fulton's two daughters, Jessie Skinner and Agnes Hare, who lived through many of the incidents that are narrated in this book and heard firsthand the stories that John Fulton told. They both worked untiringly on the necessary research and the checking of the manuscript.

My sincere thanks goes to each of these good people who have helped to make clear and plain the footprints of John Fulton, which will endure in Fiji as long as time shall last.

The phonetic spelling of Fijian words and names is used throughout this book. If the Fijian spelling is different it is given in parentheses ( ) after the first use.

Contents

John Edwin Fulton

Once Upon a Time

"—AND SO, one sunshiny day in the spring of 1857, just seventeen years ago, George Nichol Gordon and his beautiful young wife got on board the missionary ship *Day Spring* and sailed away over the ocean from Nova Scotia, this beautiful land of ours." Mother Hannah Fulton, seated in her rocking chair by the fire, was telling again the oft-asked-for story of the brave young Presbyterian missionaries to her five-year-old son, Johnny.

"Yes, Mother—and they sailed and they sailed. Go on, Mother," urged little Johnny impatiently. He knew the story by heart, but he never tired of it and never wanted even a tiny hesitation.

"All right, Johnny. They sailed and they sailed over the ocean away down past the United States, and past Brazil, and past South America."

"And around Cape Horn," added Johnny, eager to help.

"Yes, and into the Pacific Ocean, and up past the island of Tahiti, and past Samoa, till they came to the island of——"

"Erromanga in the New Hebrides!" added Johnny triumphantly.

"In Samoa," mother went on again, "they picked up two

9

Rarotongan teachers, one of whom was named Joe, and also a New Hebridean boy, whose name was Mana. He had come from Erromanga to go to school in Samoa, and was now ready to go back to his own people to help preach the gospel, for the people of Erromanga were heathen. They worshiped idols, and they were cannibals!

"When they arrived at Dillon Bay they made friends with the people by trading mirrors and cloth and fishhooks and axes for food and labor, and soon had a fairly comfortable house built on a small hill a little way from the village. They started school, cared for the sick, and preached the gospel, and it looked as if things were going to be all right when a terrible hurricane struck the island. Many native huts were blown down, and many of the gardens were destroyed, and food became scarce.

"That was bad enough, but one day a trading ship came to Dillon Bay and some of the sailors were sick with the measles. Many of the natives who came to the ship to trade came down with measles too, then it spread till there was a terrible epidemic of measles, and hundreds of people died.

" 'It's the white people's fault,' said some of the natives angrily.

" 'Yes, this is the white people's sickness,' said others who were not friendly.

" 'I wish the white people had never come here,' said another.

" 'Why don't we kill the two white teachers?'

" 'Yes! Yes! Let us kill the two white missionaries!' shouted the unfriendly ones. But all the people were not unfriendly, and the friendly ones shouted, 'No! No! The missionaries are good to us. You mustn't kill them.'

" 'But they have made our gods angry with us. We will have to kill them or our gods will never be good to us again!' shouted the unfriendly ones. And after that things began to get bad for the Gordons. Mana and Joe and six other faithful big boys came and slept in their house, and took turns keeping watch every night. Then one day Mana went to the village and overheard an old heathen named Nahobili planning with nine other people to kill the missionaries after two days.

" 'Please, Misi [Mr.] Gordon, don't stay here! Go and sleep in the village,' begged Mana. 'You have many friends there and they will protect you.' But Mr. Gordon just couldn't believe that the people would kill him after all the good he had done for them, so he wouldn't go."

Mother Fulton paused for a second. Little Johnny's heart beat faster, his eyes bugged out, he could hardly breathe. "But they did kill them, Mother, didn't they?" he whispered.

"Johnny, my son, George Nichol Gordon was every inch a brave, courageous man, and when the second day came, he had school in the morning just as usual. After school he sent eight of the big boys to cut some thatch for a new house he was building nearer to the village. Then he said, 'Mana, you stay here and help Mrs. Gordon, and Joe, you come and help me at the new house.' Then off went Mr. Gordon and Joe. They had been gone only about half an hour when Mana saw old Nahobili with eight men and a boy coming up the hill. Mrs. Gordon bravely went to the door to meet him.

" 'Where is Misi Gordon?' demanded Nahobili sullenly.

" 'He and Joe are working on the new house,' she said, trying to be pleasant. 'Can I do something for you? Would you like something to eat? or a coconut? or maybe a few fishhooks?'

" 'We want some cloth so we can come to church on Sunday,' he replied. 'We will go and ask Misi Gordon for some.' As they set off, Mrs. Gordon, overcome with concern, called out, 'Are you really going to kill Mr. Gordon?'

"The boy was the last one in the line as they went away. He answered jokingly, 'Yes, that's what we are going to do!'

"At once Mrs. Gordon told Mana to take some lunch to Mr. Gordon, and told him to keep his eye on old Nahobili. Mana hurried down the path after the men. He saw the eight men and the boy hide in the bushes. He saw old Nahobili go up to Mr. Gordon and heard him say, 'Misi, we want some cloth so we can come to church on Sunday.'

" 'All right,' said Mr. Gordon. And picking up a small piece of board, he wrote a note to his wife. 'Here, Nahobili, take this to Mrs. Gordon and she will give you the cloth,' he said.

" 'No, I want you to come and give it to me,' demanded Nahobili. 'I want some medicine for a sick man too.'

"Believing he really did want some medicine, Mr. Gordon started off up the hill with Nahobili following on behind. As they entered the bush there was a bloodcurdling yell, and one of the men who had hidden there sprang upon Mr. Gordon and slashed his arm with a tomahawk. Mr. Gordon ran forward as fast as he could but Nahobili sprang on him from behind, and with one blow from his tomahawk, cut a deep gash in his back. A second blow cut his neck and the poor man fell to the ground mortally wounded.

"Then another bad man, Ubel by name, rushed up the hill, sneaked up behind Mrs. Gordon and with one blow cut through her side, and with a second blow cut her neck. She fell on the floor, poor soul, and died right there." Mother Fulton paused as she always did at this place in the story, overcome with the sadness of the tale. Little Johnny was silent too, as he always was at this point. Then, whispering hoarsely, he asked, "Did the bad people eat them all up?"

"No, no, Johnny, the friendly ones from the village wouldn't let them. They made rough coffins for them and buried them on the riverbank, in Dillon Bay, on the island of Erromanga."

"Why did they go, Mother? Why did they go?" asked Johnny. "Didn't they know they might get killed?"

"Well, you see, God's children have the light of the gospel, and it is their business to shine that light in the dark places of the world. And of all the dark places, maybe Erromanga in the New Hebrides was the darkest. Forty years before the Gordons went to Erromanga, another brave missionary, John Williams, went to Dillon Bay. Do you want me to tell you that story too?"

"Oh, yes, Mother, of course I do," said Johnny settling down for another thrilling tale.

"Well, in 1817, John Williams and his brave wife sailed from England on another missionary ship called the *Duff*. For twenty-two years he preached the gospel in Tahiti, Raiatea, Rarotonga, and Samoa. He even built his own missionary ship and named it *The Messenger of Peace*. Well, John Williams always had a burden to preach the gospel in the New Hebrides also, so one day in 1839, leaving Mrs. Williams in Samoa, he got on a sailing ship called the *Camden* that was going to touch in at Dillon Bay on Erromanga, on its way to Australia.

"There were two other missionaries on the ship—Mr. Harris and Mr. Cunningham. When they arrived at Dillon Bay, Mr. Williams got into a small rowboat with Captain Morgan, the two other missionaries, and four sailors. A number of natives gathered on the beach. They had their spears and their tomahawks and their bows and arrows in their hands, but they did not look hostile, so the captain threw them a bundle containing a number of looking glasses. The natives looked pleased with this present, and when the men asked for some fresh water, they not only gave them water, they brought them some coconuts also. After a while the men waded ashore. At first the natives were frightened, but the captain got some cloth from the rowboat and gave them each a piece. This made some of them happy. But, unfortunately, some time before this sailors from another trading ship had mistreated the islanders, and there were some among the natives who were determined on revenge.

Suddenly there was a bloodcurdling yell and several natives rushed upon the white men, brandishing their clubs wildly. All but Mr. Harris and Mr. Williams were able to make it to the rowboat, but poor Mr. Harris and Mr. Williams were clubbed to death at the water's edge."

"Did the captain try to get their bodies?" asked Johnny fearfully.

"Yes, he tried. But the natives, yelling and shouting, dragged them away into the bush."

"And did they eat them all up, Mother?"

"Yes, Johnny, they cooked them in a hot-stone oven and ate them up. The captain told the governor about it when he reached Australia, and the governor sent a warship to Erromanga to see if they could find the bodies, but all they could find was their skulls and their bones. They took Mr. Williams' bones to his sorrowing wife in Samoa, where she buried them."

"And, Mother, did any more missionaries try to go and preach the gospel in the New Hebrides?"

"Indeed they did. In 1848, just nine years after John Williams and Mr. Harris were killed and eaten, John Geddie and his brave young wife went from here in Nova Scotia, and landed on another island in the New Hebrides called Aneityum. I was a little girl at that time, and I remember how we all took part in raising funds to build the missionary ship, the *Dayspring,* and my mother used to tell me stories about John Williams and John Geddie. Everybody called him Little Johnny Geddie, because they had known him since he was a boy."

"And did they eat him all up too, Mother?"

"No! No! God be praised, the people on Aneityum turned from their heathen ways and many of them became good Christians. The Geddies worked there for twenty-four years. He translated the Bible for them and at last died a natural death, and was given a Christian burial."

"Mother, wasn't John Geddie on Aneityum when George Gordon was killed on Erromanga?"

"That's right, laddie."

"Did the people on Erromanga ever become Christians?"

"Well, that is another sad story. But when the news of George Gordon's death came to Nova Scotia, his younger brother, James, got restless and said, 'I will not let the light go out. I must go and take George's place.' With the prayer on his lips, 'O Lord, lay not this sin to their charge,' the brave good man did go and carried on his brother's work right there at Dillon Bay on Erromanga.

"For a number of years he built mission houses, schools, and churches, and he had the joy of seeing many become Christians. Then one day he was sitting on the veranda of his house revising his translation of the book of Acts in the New Testament. He was checking over the story of the stoning of Stephen, when a heathen savage who still blamed the white missionaries for making the heathen gods angry, crept up behind him and without warning killed him with a tomahawk."

"And did they eat him all up, Mother?"

"No, no, Johnny, there were many friendly natives there, you see, and they wouldn't let the heathen eat him. They buried him like a Christian."

"But, Mother, didn't the people of Erromanga ever——"

"Be patient, laddie, I'm just coming to that. When the news of James Gordon's death reached home, another young man by the name of Hugh Robertson and his wife, from here in Nova Scotia, said, 'We're not afraid to go to bloody Erromanga. We'll go and keep the light burning,' and they did go. Soon there was not an idol left. The whole island was won for God."

Five-year-old Johnny Fulton sighed and settled back in deep satisfaction for a moment, then said, "Mother, are all the missionaries from Nova Scotia brave and courageous?"

"Of course, my son!"

"John is a good name for a missionary, isn't it, Mother?"

"Of course it is, my son."

"There was John Williams, John Geddie, and—" He paused a moment as if making up his mind.

"And—?" encouraged mother.

"And, Mother, do you think Johnny Fulton could ever be a brave courageous missionary too? Someday?"

"Of course he could, my son," his mother replied. And she lifted five-year-old Johnny onto her lap and hugged him tight.

Johnny was one of five children in the family of George and Hannah Fulton. He had two brothers, Fred and William, and a sister, Agnes, who were quite a bit older than he. His little sister, Ella, was quite a bit younger. So when Johnny was five years old, storytime at his bedtime was especially for him, and the influence of the stories of these brave Nova Scotia missionaries left an indelible impression upon his heart.

His father, George Fulton, was a housebuilder and found plenty of work in Halifax, Nova Scotia, so he was able to provide well for his family. He was of Scotch descent, and had been a Presbyterian church elder for thirty years.

Now, George Fulton had two younger brothers, Samuel and John, who had settled in Eastern United States, and a younger sister who had settled in Oakland, California. These had all come in contact with the early Seventh-day Adventist preachers, and in 1874 had just accepted the Advent message. Both Samuel and John Fulton began to preach their new-found faith at once, and in their enthusiasm wrote to their brother George in Halifax, telling him of their great joy in finding new light. They gave him scriptural proof that Saturday is the seventh day of the fourth commandment, and urged him to come out of Babylon and get ready for the second coming of Christ.

Mother Hannah Fulton was greatly impressed with these

letters, but George Fulton was only indignant. He was a Scots-
man, and had inherited a large bump of Scottish caution or
stubbornness. He wrote back giving all the arguments against
the Sabbath that he could think of. He wasn't going to be tossed
about with every wind of doctrine. He even went to the Presbyterian preachers, and got all the arguments against the Sabbath
that they could give him. However, the reply letters from
Samuel and John knocked the foundations from every argument and at last left him silent, but not convinced. He decided
that his brothers had erred from the faith, and became prejudiced
against what he thought was delusion.

During this time the aunt in Oakland also wrote letters. She
didn't preach so much in her epistles, but she enlarged on
California's sunshine and flowers and fruit. She begged them to
come and live in California, and assured them that the railroad
across country had been completed six years before, so traveling
would be easy. Her letters took effect. They made the ice and
snow and cold of Nova Scotia seem so unbearable that at last,
in 1875, when young Johnny was six years old and Ella just two
or three, George Fulton with his wife and two younger children
emigrated to Oakland, California, and rented a house there till
he could build his own home. The three older children had
elected to stay in Nova Scotia for the time being.

Now, maybe it just happened, but that very year the Pacific
Press had erected their beautiful two-story building right there
in Oakland, and the Fultons' new home was not far from it. It
also happened that before long, Elder W. M. Healey held a
series of meetings in that same town. Of course, it was only
natural for the Adventist aunt to invite George and Hannah
Fulton to attend those meetings.

Mother Fulton drank in the truth night after night, and at
last said, "George, I'm convinced the Seventh-day Adventists
are right, and I'm going to join them."

2

"Well, I'm not," said Father Fulton. "The Presbyterian faith is good enough for me."

"Well, I am," said Mother Fulton. "I always thought I was following the light from the Bible, and when I see new light shining out of the Word of God, George, I must obey it." So Mother Fulton was baptized and joined the Oakland Seventh-day Adventist church. She took young John and Ella to Sabbath school every Sabbath, and together they studied the Sabbath school lessons written by Prof. G. H. Bell.

As the months went by they heard many of the Adventist pioneers preach. They heard James White, Ellen G. White, S. N. Haskell, Uriah Smith, J. H. Waggoner, J. O. Corliss, and J. N. Loughborough. John was greatly impressed by the words and the earnestness of all of these servants of God, but as a little boy he remembered best the story J. N. Loughborough told of the beginning of the work in California.

It was in 1868, just one year before John Fulton was born, that Elder Loughborough and Elder D. T. Bourdeau arrived in San Francisco with a large tent, intending to hold meetings in many of the cities and towns. Since the transcontinental railway had not been completed at that time, they had traveled by boat from New York to Panama, across the Isthmus of Panama by train, then continued by boat to California. As soon as they landed in San Francisco they went to the home of Brother B. G. St. John, intending to talk with him about the best place to begin holding meetings.

Now just a few weeks before this, a man by the name of Wolf, who lived in the town of Petaluma, forty miles to the north, had a dream. In this dream he saw two men lighting a fire. It burned brightly and made the people happy. But the ministers in Petaluma didn't like the fire, and tried to put it out. But the harder they tried, the brighter the fire burned. It spread and spread till there were five fires. Mr. Wolf belonged to the

Independent Christian church, and he told his dream at prayer meeting.

A few days before this they had read in the newspaper that two men were coming by boat to San Francisco with a big tent in which they intended to hold meetings, and when Mr. Wolf told his dream, they said, "It might mean that these two evangelists will come and preach here in Petaluma." So they prayed, "If these, O Lord, are Thy servants, give them a prosperous journey and come Thou with them."

Then they sent one of their number, Mr. Hough, to San Francisco to see if he could find out anything about the evangelists. He went to the steamship wharf and asked, "Have the two men and the big tent we read about in the newspaper arrived yet?"

"They sure have," the men replied, "and you'll find them at Mr. St. John's house on Minna Street." Within thirty minutes Mr. Hough found the evangelists.

"Won't you please come with me to Petaluma?" he invited Elder Loughborough. "We would like to talk to you before you decide where to pitch your tent and begin holding your meetings."

Brother Loughborough felt impressed that this was God's answer to his prayers, so he said, "Yes, indeed, we will come." The next day they went to Petaluma, and Mr. Hough took the two evangelists to Mr. Wolf's place for dinner. As Mr. Wolf saw them coming through his gate he said to his wife, "Wife, they are the men! They are the very men I saw in my dream!"

So the tent was pitched in Petaluma, and the dream was literally fulfilled. The light burned brightly. The other ministers tried to stop the work, but they couldn't, and within a few years the Seventh-day Adventists did have five churches in that district.

Young John loved that story, and whenever Elder Loughborough came to visit in the Fulton home he was asked to tell

that story again and again. But Father Fulton didn't like that
story, and he didn't like any of the Adventist preachers. He
finally became very bitter. "It's no use asking me to go to any
more of those Adventist meetings," he said angrily.

"Why, George!" said mother sadly.

"And I'll never read any more of your old tracts."

"But, George!"

"I'll tell you what I'm going to do," he said. "I'm going to
move to Oregon! Even if I have just finished building our new
home. I'll sell it and I'll get as far away from the Adventists as
I can. That's what I'm going to do."

In the Wilds of Oregon

NOW THE RAILWAY from California to Oregon was not completed till 1883, so in the spring of 1877 Father George Fulton had to get on a boat at San Francisco and sail up the West Coast to Portland, Oregon. From there he took a train down to Salem.

"There are less than two hundred Seventh-day Adventists in all of Washington and Oregon put together," someone had told him. So he felt that almost anywhere in the State he would be safe from their influence. All he wanted was a place in the wilds, with a river, farm land, trees, and mountains where he could be alone. And after diligent search he found just what he wanted—a large ranch two and a half miles up the river from the town. It had several acres of good farm land suitable for growing potatoes, and there were plenty of Indians nearby who could be hired to do the work.

He bought a rowboat to keep himself in contact with the world, then set to work. He cut his poles from the woods on the side of the mountain, split his own shakes and shingles, and built his new home on a hill near a little stream that came tumbling down the side of the mountain into the larger river in the valley. It was only a humble home, but the view was magnificent! No king in his most luxurious palace ever had a better one. But best of all for Father Fulton was the thought that no Adventists would ever bother him here!

His frequent letters to Mother Fulton telling of the progress he was making on their new home in the wilds, however, brought more suffering than joy to her. She had made real friends with the Adventists in Oakland. How she would miss them! She got such real joy from attending church regularly. How she would miss going to church! The trees, the mountains, the streams that Father Fulton raved about in his letters somehow sounded so lonely to her, and many were her regrets over her husband's decision.

But there was possibly one good thing about this discouraging prospect. Young John's worldly companions in public school were little by little leading him astray. Already she had smelled tobacco on him several times and even had caught him smoking more than once. Perhaps up there in the wilds it would be easier for him to live a clean life. Yes, maybe after all, Providence was leading. It might be a good move for her boy. So Mother Fulton kept her poise, praying, hoping for the best.

At last, in the spring of 1878, when John was almost nine years old and sister Ella about five, father was all ready for them. So Mother Fulton and the two children emigrated to Oregon also. The grandeur of the scenery was all that father had described and more! The running streams with thousands of salmon in the spawning season, with their red-and-silver sides gliding over the shallows and rapids; the great dense forests of fir, alder, and maple, interspersed with wild berry bushes; the glorious birds with their tuneful songs; the graceful deer tripping through the shrubs; the cumbersome bears feeding greedily on the wild berries—all these combined to make of this new home a paradise on earth.

John and Ella romped together among the trees and played

in the babbling brooks. Every day they brought home some exciting story of seeing a startled deer with its great antlers leap away from them like a streak. Without a doubt, it was a good place for a boy to grow up. And better still was the fact that the boys in the new country school where John now attended were not tempted with the tobacco habit, and John soon forgot all about the filthy stuff. Yet with all of its advantages, for mother there was an overhanging, all-pervading sense of solitude.

Mother Fulton secretly hoped that father's hostility toward the truth would soften and perhaps even disappear. Often she would casually leave a copy of the *Signs of the Times* on a chair near the fireplace, hoping he might pick it up and read. But not he! To show her that he saw through her devices, and convince her that it was no use trying, he wouldn't deign to touch the paper with his hands, but would pick it up with the fire tongs and throw it into the fire. Mother Fulton remained sweet and patient through it all. However, his belligerent attitude, the solitude, and the loneliness gnawed continually at her heart.

During the first winter in Oregon little Ella came down with rheumatic fever. The two and a half miles from town by rowboat were so difficult that no doctor from the city would come to such a remote place. Father had to be away all day plowing in the field and John was away all day at school, so mother had to stay at home alone and look after her sick daughter. But she was not alone and friendless. God had promised, "I will never leave thee, nor forsake thee." Instinctively she reached for her Bible and opened it by chance to James 5. Or was it by chance? Anyway there were the words—they seemed specially illuminated for her: "Is any sick among you? . . . let them pray over him, anointing him with oil in the name of the Lord: and the prayer of faith shall save the sick, and the Lord shall raise him up."

"Ella!" called Mother Fulton, trying to suppress her excitement. "Just listen to these words in the Bible." And she read the verses from James 5 aloud to her sick little daughter. "Ella dear, do you believe that Jesus could heal you if I anointed you with oil and prayed for you?"

"Yes, Mother, I do," said Ella.

"Then let us do what Jesus tells us to do," said Mother Fulton. She took some oil and anointed Ella's forehead and prayed. God honored their faith, and little Ella, who had been in bed for weeks, got right up and walked! She even went to meet her father as he came back from the field that evening. Father Fulton could not believe his eyes. God had performed a miracle for his little girl and for his good wife, and *they* were Adventists! Could she be right after all? he wondered. The thought lingered uncomfortably in his mind for many days.

One day soon after this, Father Fulton came in and announced, "Well, Mother, it looks as though we are going to have some neighbors."

"Some neighbors?" asked Mother Fulton in surprise. "Whatever makes you think that?"

"Well, there's a man camping on the place next to ours," father replied, "and it looks to me as though he plans to build."

There was indeed a man camping on the place next to theirs. To make sure, Father Fulton strolled over to chat with him.

"Sure I'm going to build here," answered the man. "I like it here—beautiful scenery and all that, but it's wild and isolated, and I like roughing it. My wife is coming up next week. She likes roughing it too."

The neighbor's wife did come up, and Mother Fulton went over to see her. When she returned from her visit there was a curious smile on her face.

"Do you like the new neighbors?" father asked as they sat down to dinner that night.

"I surely do," mother replied with that curious smile.

"What makes you so happy about them?" asked father getting a little suspicious.

"Well, Father, I might as well tell you now, for you'll find out sooner or later. They are Seventh-day Adventists."

"Seventh-day Adventists!" gasped father. His face blanched. After a long pause he finally said, "To think—I couldn't get away from them, even here!"

But that wasn't all. The new neighbors were wonderful folks. Father couldn't help liking them. They were just his kind of people, and they soon became fast friends. It wasn't long before they announced that Elder Alonzo T. Jones was going to hold a series of meetings in town.

"George, wouldn't you and Hannah and the children like to come with us to the meetings?" they invited.

"I'd like to go very much," said mother.

"So would we," chorused John and Ella.

With apparent reluctance father said, "All right, then, I'll take you. But," he added, "you needn't think I'm going to become an Adventist. I'll never do that."

Night after night they got into their little rowboat and father rowed them the two and a half miles to the meetings, and two and a half miles back home again. In spite of his hard feelings, he liked young Elder Jones. He liked his scholarly appearance. He liked his sparkling presentation of the doctrines. He even invited him to spend two or three weeks with him at the ranch. Elder Jones and his wife proved to be pleasant guests. Mrs. Jones helped Mother Fulton with the housework and the cooking. Elder Jones rolled up his sleeves and helped father with the milking and the farmwork. To John's and Ella's delight, he practiced his voice culture every morning in the nearby woods. And as he ohed and ahed till his voice echoed and re-echoed through the valley, the children ohed and ahed with him and danced up and down with delight.

On occasion father discussed and even argued with Elder Jones over the doctrines he was preaching, but always in a tactful way Elder Jones proved to be too good a match for him. The Spirit of God was striving with father, and He gave him no rest day or night, till finally one day in 1879, while chopping wood, he threw down his ax, strode into the house, and with tears flowing down his cheeks, he said, "Hannah, I can't stand it any longer. I know it's the truth. I can't run away from it. I can't fight it. I'm going to give in and become an Adventist with you." And he did.

Great was the happiness that came to the Fulton home away up there in the wilds of Oregon. It wasn't lonely for Mother Fulton anymore, for now she not only had Adventist neighbors but every Sabbath day the Fulton family rowed together two and a half miles down the river to the little church that had been organized in Salem.

The years that followed were happy, prosperous years. Father and his Indian workmen—or perhaps more accurately, Indian squaws—did well in the potato business. Meanwhile young John grew to be a tall gangling youth. Ella also grew up and was soon old enough to accompany John to school. And the walk to the river and the two and a half miles by rowboat there and back each day made them both strong and rugged. When not in school John worked more and more on the farm with his father, and each year brought new evidences that God was with them.

One night when John was fourteen years old there was a terrible storm. The lightning flashed, the thunder roared, and the rain pelted down. Father Fulton got up about midnight and went to check on the horses and cows in the barn. The flashes of lightning lighted up the whole mountainside behind the house, and made a patch of giant fir trees that had been killed in a forest fire many years before stand out like an army of ghosts, waving their naked arms menacingly toward him.

Suddenly there was a terrifying crack as a bolt of lightning struck one of those ghostlike giants. It crashed to the ground. The top of the tree was pinned to the ground where it fell by the branches, but the bottom part, a log sixty feet long and six feet thick, broke off and began rolling down the steep mountainside toward the house. There was no time for Father Fulton to warn mother, Ella, and John, who were in the house. The log gathered momentum as it rolled, shearing off the smaller trees and flattening out the shrubs and bushes that were in its way. The house lay directly in its path.

"O God save them!" cried Father Fulton. He closed his eyes in an effort to shut out the scene as his house would be crushed like matchwood and the lives of his loved ones snuffed out if God did not intervene. Then a miracle happened. As that log came thundering down, one end stuck momentarily in a large clump of green trees and deflected it just enough to miss the house as it continued on its course of destruction and finally came to rest in a hollow.

Trembling with emotion, Father Fulton rushed into the house and told his loved ones of their miraculous escape. Then while the storm raged outside they offered fervent prayers of praise and thanksgiving to God for preserving their lives and property.

In the morning the storm had passed over. The family rose early, and as they gazed wide-eyed at the track the log had left on the mountainside, veering just before it hit the house, goose pimples came out all over them. For a moment no one could speak, then father said, "God must love us."

"Yes," agreed mother, "and God must need us. He must have a work for each of us to do."

"Mother," said John with awe in his voice, "could it be that God wants *me* to be a worker for Him? And that's why He saved *my* life?"

"What else could it be, my son?"

"Maybe a missionary to Erromanga?"

"Who can tell where it will be, my son?"

"Then, Mother, I must go to Healdsburg College just as soon as I am old enough."

"Son, that's why Healdsburg College was established just last year—to train young people to be preachers and missionaries."

"That's what I am going to do then, Mother. I'm going to Healdsburg just as soon as I am old enough," said John emphatically. And from that day there was a new determination seen in everything that he did.

For years that giant log remained unmoved in the hollow below their house, continually bearing mute testimony to the fact that "the angel of the Lord encampeth round about them that fear him, and delivereth them."

During these years the West was developing rapidly. Every year thousands of immigrants from every walk of life settled in California, Oregon, and Washington. Among them were John Fulton's two older brothers and his older sister. They were all married by this time. Fred Fulton settled in San Diego, and was an engineer connected with the water company there. Will Fulton, also an engineer, settled in Castro Valley and was connected with the Contra Costa Water Company at Lake Chabot. His sister Agnes, now Mrs. Orchard, settled in Oakland.

Meanwhile the Seventh-day Adventist message was also making encouraging progress all up and down the West Coast. More and more ministers were arriving. Evangelistic tent meetings were being held and new churches were being organized in many places. Among the ministers who were sent to Oregon about this time were Father George Fulton's two brothers, Samuel and John. How thrilled they were to find their brother George in the truth at last, and how thrilled they were to hear young John Fulton say, "Uncle John and Uncle Samuel, I have decided to become a minister too. Maybe a missionary to Erromanga. And I'm going to Healdsburg College when I am seventeen."

"God bless you, my boy," said Uncle Samuel, "I'm sure you will make a good minister!"

Another of the ministers who came to Oregon was Elder C. L. Boyd. In fact, he was president of the North Pacific Conference from 1882 to 1887, but that did not stop him from holding tent meetings. All he needed was a young man to look after the tent, lead the singing, and help with the visiting. Among the young men who were his tentmasters, as they were called in those days, was a young man twenty-two years old, by the name of John Martin Cole. He joined Elder Boyd in 1884 and was with him for about two years.

Young John Fulton followed the news of the tent missions with great interest and in his mind he often played with the thought—*John* Williams and *John* Geddie were good missionaries. Maybe *John* Cole and *John* Fulton will be good missionaries too, someday! Who can tell? Maybe they will. Why not?

In 1885 when young John Fulton was sixteen years old he was baptized. The next year, when he was seventeen years old— a young giant six feet four inches tall, who wore size twelve shoes —he went to Healdsburg College. And who do you think was one of the first students he met there—John Martin Cole, now twenty-four years old.

"Why, John Cole, whatever are you doing here?" John Fulton asked in surprise.

"I'm preparing to be a minister to help preach the third angel's message," said John Cole. "And you?"

"I am too," replied John Fulton humbly. "Or maybe a missionary to Erromanga. I've wanted to be a missionary to Erromanga ever since I was five years old, and my mother used to tell me stories about John Williams, John Geddie, and the Gordons."

"Oh!"

"Say, John, did you ever notice how many missionaries have been named *John?* It seems to me that *Johns* make good missionaries. I sure want to be one. How about you?"

"Yes, indeed," John Cole replied. "I would be willing to go anywhere for God."

"I would too," said John Fulton. And their hearts were knit together from that moment.

There was another student that John Fulton took a great liking to. It was Robert Hare, a twenty-seven-year-old Irishman from New Zealand. He had been in college most of the preceding year. His full black beard and serious manner made him different from the others. He was from New Zealand, and that was near the Pacific islands. He could tell him much about life away down under! John wanted him for a friend. So as soon as he could, he approached Robert and warmly shook his hand. "Robert, I'm so glad to meet you. My name is John Fulton. I'm from the wilds of Oregon, and I'm here to prepare myself to be a missionary somewhere—maybe to Erromanga in the New Hebrides. Someday I would like you to tell me all you know about life down under in the isles of the South Pacific."

Robert looked into the honest face of this clean-shaved giant. For all his size he was still a lad, ten years younger than he. But the warmth of the grasp of his hand and the earnestness of his words told him they were friends already. And he replied, "That I will, Johnny my lad. That I will!" And he did.

But life was not all sunshine and roses for John at college. Some of the younger fellows tried to have many a joke at the expense of this young man from the wilds of Oregon.

"Say, Mr. Fulton," said one, "could you by any chance be

related to Paul Bunyan, maybe?" And his friends laughed uproariously.

"Say, Mr. Fulton, just how long do you think a man's legs ought to be?" inquired another.

"Ha! Ha! Ha! Ha!" laughed the others.

"And say, Mr. Fulton, what size shoes do you wear?" asked another.

And while the others were holding their sides, another added, "John Fulton will sure leave huge footprints in the sands of time."

"Ha! Ha! Ha! Ha! He sure will. He sure will." The other young fellows joined in.

Robert couldn't help hearing what was going on. "Take no notice of them, Johnny my lad," he said one day. "They'll soon get tired of their nonsense. When I first came, some of the students thought that because I came from New Zealand I would be a Maori with a tattooed face! Some of them laughed. But I just smiled and said, 'Did you ever hear tell of a Maori with a beard like mine? When you young fellows can grow a beard as good as this one, then you can laugh all you want.' And that was the end of it."

John got the idea. He put up with the bantering for a day or two more. Then one day after a repetition of these crude jokes, while they were preparing the vegetables in the kitchen, he turned around and said, "Well, fellows, if you really want to know, I might as well tell you. No, I am not related to Paul Bunyan, but I think a fellow's legs ought to be long enough to reach the ground." Then lifting his foot and placing it on a chair right before them, he added, "And I take size twelve. Moreover I intend to do my best to leave some worthy footprints somewhere on the sands of time. Now, how many of you *little* boys can match that? Well there you are. Now laugh as much as you want to."

There was a stifled murmur among the boys. For a moment work on the vegetables stopped. Somehow they didn't want to laugh anymore. Their jokes didn't sound funny. Then someone volunteered, "You win, John."

At this everybody smiled his approval, and that was the end of the jokes. John Fulton was accepted in college.

Ordained and Sent Forth

LET US GO BACK for a few moments to the year 1869. It was a wonderful year in many ways. It was the year John Fulton was born, and not the least of the marvelous things that happened that year was the completion of the transcontinental railway linking the East of the United States with the West. This opened the way for hundreds and thousands of people to emigrate to the West. So it happened that the following year, 1870, a young man by the name of James Nimrod Newlon with his beautiful young wife, Josephine, moved West and located in a little settlement named Bishop, in Owens Valley, California. He was fortunate in obtaining a splendid section of land suitable for wheat, sheep, and cattle, and quickly settled down to the rugged life of the early pioneers.

The following year on April 4, 1871, a baby girl came to brighten their home. There was no doctor in the settlement, but one of the older experienced women acted as midwife. Labor was long and difficult, and when at last the baby arrived, the midwife took one look and gasped, "I'm afraid she will never live, Josephine. She's blue. No circulation! Anyway, your life is more important than hers." With that she placed the little blue baby girl on a chair, and turned to the care of the mother.

3

In a few seconds, however, that little blue baby girl let out a yell loud enough and long enough to tell the world she was very much alive.

"She's alive!" cried Josephine with joy. "Here, give her to me." As she cuddled her to her heart, she murmured, "I'm going to call her Susie, after my mother, and Virginia, after the virgin Queen Elizabeth for whom my home State of Virginia was named."

"And, Josephine," added the midwife, "you have no idea how important Susie Virginia is. She has made history today. She is the first white baby girl to be born in Bishop!"

When Susie was two years old, a baby brother, Ben, was added to the family. For seven years after that, life went on according to the usual pioneer pattern, with its ups and downs, its good years and its bad years.

When Susie was about nine years old, after two poor years in succession, Mr. Newlon decided to try somewhere else, so he rented out his ranch and moved with his little family to Los Angeles, and took over a ten-acre farm near Hollywood on what is now Vernon Avenue. They had not been there long when Elder Healey, the same preacher who had brought Mother Fulton into the truth about five years before, held a series of meetings nearby, and Mrs. Newlon and Susie accepted the truth and were charter members of the first Seventh-day Adventist church in Los Angeles! Mr. Newlon did not join the church at that time.

After two or three years in Los Angeles he decided to go back to his ranch in Bishop. So he sold the ten-acre farm for a song, to a man who later divided it into lots and made a fortune out of it.

But James Nimrod Newlon obtained far greater riches than that, for in 1885, when the first church in the Owens Valley was organized in Bishop, he, his wife, and his daughter were all charter members of that church. Susie Virginia was fourteen years old at this time, and she and her mother often had long serious talks about the future.

"Susie, what do you think you'd like to be when you grow up?" asked her mother one day. "A teacher? a nurse? or a——"

"Or a what?" broke in Susie eagerly.

"Well, you know Susie," said mother. "Or a teacher's wife, or a preacher's wife, or a ——"

"I'd rather be a missionary's wife, Mother," replied Susie without any hesitation.

"And go far away across the ocean to some mission field?"

"Yes! Far away, to Africa or to China."

"You would?"

"Well, someone must go. Mustn't they, Mother?"

"Of course!"

"Well?"

"Well then, Susie, as soon as you are old enough you should plan to take the nurse's course at the St. Helena Sanitarium, or the teacher's course at Healdsburg College, or——"

"It will be the teacher's course at Healdsburg College, Mother," said Susie without hesitation. "That's where I want to go."

"Then in the meantime, my dear, you must learn all you can about teaching right here at the country school, and you must learn all you can about cooking and housework right here in the home."

"Yes, Mother, I will," said Susie eagerly. "I will." And Susie did.

At last in 1887, when she was sixteen, Susie Virginia Newlon went to Healdsburg College. She was not merely another country girl student. She was sweet sixteen, graceful, vivacious, and beautiful. Henrietta Johnson, the mathematics teacher, loved her right away and took her under her wing. Susie sat at Henrietta's table and she soon began to get acquainted with the other students. There were the Chinnock twins, Julia and Clara, so sparkling and sweet. There were Jessie Yarnell, Mary Lockwood, Ollie McElhaney, Lily Otis, and many others. Also Alma Baker, who later married E. L. McKibbin and became the famous church school teacher and textbook writer, and Jessie Creamer, who later married John Paap, who was one of the principals of Avondale College in Australia and also one of the pioneer professors of Pacific Union College.

Among the young men who stood out in her girlish opinion, were Herbert Lacey, Herbert Dexter, Frank Thorp, Frank Otis, Frank Burg, Robert Hare (the Irishman from New Zealand), and John Fulton, the young giant from Oregon.

Susie loved everybody and she loved the college, and was soon wrapped up in every detail of the school program. Now you must remember, in those days the young men and the young ladies were not permitted to have anything to do with one another. They were not even allowed to talk to one another. They were not allowed to write to one another. How they managed to fall in love and get married after they graduated is a deep unsolved mystery. Of course, they could *look* at one another and there might have been some strange magic "by which one mind another mind divines." And of course, in the dining room they could discuss the events of the day at their tables. Then there was one more opportunity, and Cupid surely made the most of it.

No dishes were washed on Sabbath. But Saturday evening after the sun had set, the boys were permitted to wash the dishes while the girls wiped them and put them away. Of course, several teachers were there to supervise, but as you can imagine, there was so much clatter and so much noise and so much activity, that it was not at all impossible for a young man to say a few friendly words to a young lady, and

not the least improbable that she would say a few friendly
words back to him.

And so——well, anyway, Susie loved wiping dishes on Saturday nights and sweet, vivacious, adorable Susie had many
friendly words spoken to her by more than one of the young
men on these heartwarming occasions, and she looked forward
to them all week long.

One day soon after Susie's arrival, the principal announced,
"You will all be glad to know that Brother John I. Tay is to
spend the coming weekend with us. You will recall that he
had a most remarkable visit to Pitcairn Island last year." Immediately a murmur of excitement swept over the students. Of
course they had *heard* of John I. Tay's remarkable visit to Pitcairn, but to have the privilege of *seeing* him, and *hearing* the
story from his own lips, this was almost too good to be true.
And they talked of little else the rest of that week.

At last the weekend came, and with it John I. Tay. The
students listened breathlessly as he told of his interest in Pitcairn Island ever since he had read the book *Mutiny on the
Bounty.* When he was forty-one years old he became a Seventh-
day Adventist and at once began to dream of taking the message to the Pitcairn islanders. During the following years on
several occasions literature was sent to Pitcairn, but no replies
ever came back. Finally, last year, in 1886, when he was fifty-
four years old, his desire to take the truth to them was so great
that he worked his way as a ship's carpenter and after many
adventures landed on Pitcairn on October 18. He spent five
weeks there with the people. They had indeed received the
literature and had read it, and now with the help of the Holy
Spirit they all—one hundred and twenty seven, including the
children—decided to keep the Sabbath. They wanted him to
baptize them, but he was only a deacon, and so he had come
back to the United States to plead that an ordained minister

be sent to them at once. He ended his talk with the appeal, "Jesus said to His disciples, 'Lift up your eyes, and look on the fields; for they are white already to harvest.' My dear students, the islands of the South Pacific are indeed ready for the harvest. May God roll the burden upon some of you to go and gather in the precious sheaves."

"What did you think of that, John Cole?" breathed John Fulton to his seatmate as the meeting came to a close.

"I'll go if God calls me," whispered John Cole. "I surely will."

"So will I," whispered back John Fulton. "And say, John, did it strike you that Brother Tay's name is John? I'll tell you it's true. *Johns* make good missionaries!"

That Saturday night maybe it just happened that Susie Virginia Newlon was wiping the dishes that John Fulton was washing. "What did you think of Brother Tay's talk today, Susie?" asked John.

"It stirred my heart till I felt I could hardly wait till I graduated so that I could go to the mission field," replied Susie seriously.   •

"It did?" said John, so taken by surprise that he hardly knew what else to say.

"Yes, it did. I've always wanted to be a missionary," confided Susie.

"You have? But you're a girl," said John. "They would never send you as a missionary all by yourself."

"Who said I would have to go all by myself?" said Susie with a sly little glance that left John speechless for a moment. He looked down at the dishes that he was washing and tried to think of something to say, and when he looked up, Susie was gone. But something had happened. For a moment she was gone from his sight, but from then on she would never be gone from his heart.

Later the students were stunned by the tragic news of the death of Elder A. J. Cudney. As a result of John I. Tay's pleading, the General Conference decided to send Elder Cudney to Pitcairn in order to baptize the believers there and organize them into a church. He outfitted a schooner, the *Phebe Chapman,* and set sail from Honolulu in July, but he was never heard from again. After six months it seemed quite certain that the ship and all on board had been lost at sea. The tragedy cast a gloom over the whole student body. But it did not extinguish the missionary zeal in their hearts.

"It doesn't mean that every missionary who sails the seven seas will be lost at sea," declared John Cole. "It would take more than that to stop me."

And Robert Hare, the Irishman from New Zealand, added, "We may be called upon to suffer with Him, but remember we shall also be glorified with Him."

We must briefly pass over the events of the next two years. That year, 1887, Uncle John Fulton was elected president of the North Pacific Conference, but being an evangelist at heart, he persuaded the brethren to let his brother, Samuel Fulton, administer the conference. So Uncle Samuel became president for two years. However, in 1889 he became ill and it was necessary for him to go to the St. Helena Sanitarium, where, after getting better, he became chaplain and Bible teacher for a number of years. When Uncle Samuel left Oregon, Uncle John Fulton resumed the presidency of the North Pacific Conference for the rest of 1889 and 1890.

During the summer vacations of 1886 and 1887 Robert Hare held evangelistic meetings in Blue Lake and Arcata, California. In the summer of 1887 John Cole assisted in an evangelistic effort in Oregon, while during the summers of 1887, 1888, and 1889, young John Fulton canvassed. He sold many copies of Uriah Smith's *Thoughts on Daniel and the Revelation,* and in 1888 he sold *The Great Controversy,* which was just off the press.

In May, 1888, at the close of the school year Robert Hare and John Cole completed their course of studies. Robert was ordained May 22, and the same day he and Henrietta Johnson were married, and the next day they set sail for New Zealand. As Robert said good-by to young John Fulton, he said, "Well, John, keep your eyes on the great mission field down under."

"I certainly will, Robert," John replied.

"And who knows? Maybe someday you will be called to preach in New Zealand with me."

"Nothing would please me more," replied John fervently.

John Cole was called to Oregon, where he was ordained, and married Fanny S. Clark early in 1890. As John Cole said good-by to John Fulton he said, "Well, John, you have two more years in school. You will still be a very young man when you finish, but I'd love to have you come and help me preach in Oregon."

"Wherever the Lord calls," said John, "that's where I want to be. But you must remember, John, *we* are going to be missionaries someday far across the sea."

"I'll remember," John Cole answered warmly. And so the three friends parted.

Meanwhile at the heart-warming dishwashing sessions on Saturday nights the friendship between John Fulton and Susie Newlon blossomed.

"John Cole wants me to go to Oregon to help him preach when I'm through college," whispered John one evening as he scrubbed the pots and pans scrupulously.

"He does?" Susie whispered back.

"Yes, and Robert wants me to come to New Zealand to preach."

"He does? And where would you rather go?"

"Me? Let *me* ask where would *you* rather go."

"Me rather go? Why ask me?"

"Well, you said you wanted to be a missionary, didn't you?"

"Sure."

"And you know you can't go alone."

"Of course not!"

"Well, I want to be a missionary too, and *I* can't go alone. I would need someone to help me wash dishes, you know."

"John Fulton!" Susie's heart was pounding but she managed to say, "It's not where you want to go, John. It's where the Lord calls you, and you know it."

Then she changed the subject quickly as eighteen-year-old young ladies can do. "I am going to miss Henrietta terribly. She has been just like a big sister to me."

"Well," John suggested playfully, "maybe I could take you to New Zealand someday to see her."

"John Fulton!" she scolded impishly. "How dare you!" But the radiant glance that came with the words sent John back to his room with a song in his heart, when the dishes were done. And I wonder if he purposely chose the plural pronouns when he wrote in Susie's autograph album about that time:

"To Susie,

"However splendid our abilities may be, we will be successful only by intense application.

> "Your schoolmate,
>
> "John Edwin Fulton."

The year 1890 was John Fulton's last year in college. As that year dawned, the Spirit of God inspired the whole world family of 34,000 Seventh-day Adventist Sabbath school members with a missionary zeal unheard of before.

John I. Tay, who had been used by God to convert the Pitcairn islanders in 1886, and who had been overwhelmed by the death of Elder A. J. Cudney in 1888, simply could not rest. "We need to send missionaries *now* to the ripened harvest

Right:
A Fijian guard
at Government House.

Below:
A typical Fijian
village on
the Singatoka River.

fields of the South Pacific Islands," he pleaded everywhere he went. "We should have our own mission ship to take our own missionaries where they need to go." And at last his enthusiasm set the hearts of our people on fire. By 1890 they raised $12,000 toward the building of a mission ship. It was called the *Pitcairn.*

In the midst of this excitement John Fulton graduated from college and was first called to Crescent City, California, to assist in a series of meetings. Susie still had one more year to go before she would graduate. "But one little year won't be very long," comforted John as he said good-by. And indeed that school year was so full of excitement that it did pass quickly.

To begin with, the *Pitcairn* sailed away on October 20, 1890, with a gallant crew, a great supply of literature, beans, and dried fruit, and three missionary families. They sailed straight for Pitcairn Island where they arrived November 25. Elder and Mrs. E. H. Gates were stationed there, and soon eighty-two of the islanders were baptized and a church was organized. Elder and Mrs. A. J. Reed were next stationed at Tahiti, and later on during the next year, 1891, John I. Tay and his good wife were stationed at Suva, in Fiji.

In the spring of 1891, after a successful effort in Crescent City, John Fulton was called to assist Elder John M. Cole in holding an effort in Drain, Oregon. Their happiness at being together again can only be imagined. But when, after graduating in May of that year, Susie Virginia Newlon also came to Drain, Oregon, and on July 25 was united in marriage to John Fulton by Elder John M. Cole, John's happiness was full to overflowing.

"I knew you needed someone to wipe the dishes for you," murmured Susie happily after the service. "And do you, John Fulton, promise to help me to wash the dishes also, till death doth us part?"

John smiled, "I do."

The effort in Drain proved successful, and during the winter the workers gave Bible studies in the homes of the new believers and established them in the truth.

By February of the next year, 1892, the sad news that John I. Tay had passed away on January 8, in Suva, Fiji, after five short months of service there came as a terrible shock to them all. "Someone must go and take his place," said John Cole.

"I wish it could be me," said John Fulton.

"But you're not ordained yet, John. It must be me!" said John Cole. "I'm going to write to the General Conference and volunteer to take John Tay's place."

"Tell them I will go too if they need me," added John Fulton.

In May of that year John took Susie to spend a few weeks with Mother Newlon in Bishop, California. Yes, you've guessed it. On May 24, a lovely little baby girl was born. They named her Jessie Edwina—Jessie after Susie's favorite roommate, Jessie Creamer, and Edwina after John's second name, Edwin. And little Jessie filled their home with sunshine and their hearts with joy.

When they returned to Drain they found John and Fanny Cole overflowing with excitement. "We've been accepted! We've been accepted!" shouted John, "and we are to sail on the second trip that the *Pitcairn* makes to the South Pacific, sometime in January of next year."

"Wonderful! Wonderful!" shouted John and Susie together. "We wish we were going with you."

The following months were full of preparation. In addition to binding off the effort in Drain, the Coles were getting ready for their trip to the islands, and the Fultons were getting ready to move to Mount Vernon, Washington, where John was to hold an effort alone.

On January 8, 1893, the *Pitcairn* set sail again with another load of precious missionaries. Elder and Mrs. J. B. Cady, Elder and Mrs. E. C. Chapman, Dr. M. G. Kellogg, Miss Hattie André, and Elder and Mrs. J. M. Cole. They all had their places of service assigned. Elder and Mrs. Cole were to spend one year on Norfolk Island and then go on to Fiji. They were missionaries at last!

"Our turn will come next," said John and Susie as they said good-by. "Keep on praying for us, and we will keep praying for you."

John and Susie entered into their effort at Mount Vernon with a will. Baby Jessie grew like a weed, and by the time she was a year old she was walking around everywhere. In the month of November, 1893, John and Susie made another trip to Mother Newlon's home in Bishop, and—you've guessed it again. Jessie got a baby sister. They named her Agnes Thresa, and she was the sweetest baby girl you ever heard tell about.

Back to Mount Vernon they went, and you should have heard John preach. He was only twenty-five years old, but he was a college graduate and the father of two lovely children, and the people came to hear him gladly.

Then suddenly one day in May, 1894, a letter came from the General Conference. "I wonder what it is about?" said Susie, half suspecting what it was.

"I'll soon tell you," said John as he tore open the envelope.

"Susie, this is it," he said, and he read aloud, " 'Elder Daniells in New Zealand has put in a call for you to join their staff of workers as an evangelist. We have followed your work with great satisfaction, and believing that God has called you to the work of preaching the third angel's message, we have recommended you for ordination at the coming camp meeting. And we would like you to leave as soon after that as you can.' " John paused to breathe and to make sure it was true, and while he did, Susie added, "John, Robert Hare has had a finger in this pie. Don't you think so? Of course we will go."

"Yes, Robert most likely started the ball rolling," he agreed.

Everything went according to plan. John Edwin Fulton was ordained to the ministry at the camp meeting, and in September, when Jessie was two and a half years old, and Agnes was ten months, they set sail for New Zealand.

Among the friends who came to San Francisco to see them off was Uncle Samuel Fulton from the St. Helena Sanitarium. Waiting for a few moments till they could be alone, Uncle Samuel placed his hand lovingly on John's shoulder and said, "John, you are going to one of the ends of the earth to preach the gospel. Be humble. Always remember the power is not yours. The power belongs to God. Don't forget, John, the Bible says, 'Believe in the Lord your God, so shall ye be established; believe his prophets, so shall ye prosper.' I thank God that He has given this Adventist Movement a prophet. I don't know what we could have done without God's servant, Sister Ellen G. White. She has not only been used of God to direct this movement in the establishing of schools, sanitariums, and publishing houses, but God has used her to write letters that have inspired, encouraged, and lifted workers out of their moments of despair and discouragement.

"Sister White wrote me a letter like that once. It was in 1890, the year you graduated from college. I was sick in the sanitarium, and I was discouraged. Then this letter came. Let me read you a sentence or two from it. 'My much-respected brother in the Lord, I am afflicted as I learn of your affliction. . . . You have the pledged word of Jehovah, "Lo, I am with you alway, even unto the end of the world." . . . In the weak state of your body, the enemy may try to make his voice heard that the Lord does not love you. Oh, He *does* love you. . . . *I* have *evidence the very best* that God loves you. He will not thrust you from

Him in your weakness, for He loves you. Do not worry yourself out of the arms of Jesus, but just repose in restful quietude in His love. . . . The cloud may appear dark to you at times in itself, but when filled with the bright light of Jesus, it is turned to the brightness of gold, for the glory of God is upon it' [Letter 31, 1890. Italics in the original.]."

Uncle Samuel paused for a moment then added, "John, I cannot tell you how much good that letter did me, and look, I want you to have a copy of it. Hardship, loneliness, and sickness may come to you also. Who can tell? When the dark clouds appear take this letter out and read it, and maybe you will find that the clouds will be turned to the brightness of gold for you too."

John took the letter from his uncle's hand and put it in his pocket. "Thank you, Uncle, thank you!" he said. "I will keep it forever." And he did.

The gong sounded. The whistle blew. The gangplank was taken down. The ropes were untied. The tugboats pushed the little steamer away from the wharf. John and Susie waved and waved to their friends, and wept. They waved and wept till they were too far away to see them clearly. Then through the Golden Gate toward the golden sunset went the ship.

John and Susie Fulton and their two little girls, Jessie and Agnes, were on their way to the mission field at last!

"You're Only a Boy!"

AS THE LITTLE SHIP steamed bravely over the wide expanse of the Pacific Ocean, through calm and through storm, John and Susie had ample time to reminisce on the events of the past and to anticipate the events of the future.

"Well, I suppose father and mother will soon be living in Oakland again," said John.

"He's going to build a little cottage on your brother Will's place in the Castro Valley, isn't he?" put in Susie.

"Yes. He's getting close to three score and ten years of age now and his days of growing potatoes are over."

"They say he sold his ranch near Salem for a song!"

"Yes, he did, to two Englishmen. Dear old dad, he loved the simple old-fashioned way of life. Did I ever tell you what he said when he first heard a phonograph?"

"No."

"Well, he listened spellbound for a moment, then he looked aghast at mother and said, 'Hannah, it's possessed!' "

They laughed together for a few moments, then John continued: "Let me see, it must be pretty near two years since John and Fanny Cole sailed away in the *Pitcairn* for Norfolk Island."

"Yes, and I hear they have had good success among the Pitcairn islanders who settled there."

"John Cole would have good success anywhere."

"And they have had a baby girl, Ruita, while on Norfolk."

"That's right. And they are soon to go to Fiji, I understand."

"I wonder if we will ever see them again?"

"I wonder too! I had always hoped that our call to New Zealand would mean that we would be working with Robert and Henrietta Hare."

"But they have been called to Australia. So has Brother Daniells. There will be no one that we know to meet us when we get there."

"Well, there is Edward Hare, you know. He is the one Elder Haskell stayed with in Auckland, when he first went to New Zealand nine years ago. He was actually the first one to accept the truth there, and it was he who took Elder Haskell to the rest of the Hare family in Kaeo, one hundred and sixty miles north of Auckland. It was there that Robert accepted the truth. I understand Edward has charge of the canvassing work in New Zealand, and he and his workers have sold thousands of copies of the *Great Controversy*."

"That sounds good. That means Edward Hare will be at the wharf to meet us, and *he* will be glad to see us."

"If he is anything like Robert Hare, he will be," said John.

The ship sailed on and on, past Hawaii, past Samoa, past Fiji, and at last arrived in Auckland, New Zealand, and Edward Hare, an Irishman with a full, well-groomed beard, *was* there to meet them. He was one of the older brothers of Robert Hare, John's dear friend, and in the prime of life at forty-seven years of age.

John and Susie noticed that the welcome seemed a bit formal. Little was said till they were all through customs and were comfortably seated in Edward Hare's home. Then Edward rose and faced John. He looked him up and down, noticed his giant frame and his clean-shaven face and said, "Do you know, Mr. Fulton, we called for a preacher. But you're only a boy!"

His words cut deep into their feelings. Susie bit her lip to keep back the tears. John's face went red. Even little Jessie and baby Agnes felt the coldness of the atmosphere and clung to their mother's skirts. It took John two or three seconds to recover, then squaring his shoulders and lifting his chin, he said, "Brother Edward, true I'm only twenty-five years old, but in God's book I read of a stripling who kept so close to God that God helped him to slay a giant. And, Brother Edward, I intend to keep so close to God that He can help me to do His work too."

Now it was Edward Hare's turn to be nonplused. He had not expected such a reply. He kept his gaze on John for a few moments. So this was the young man whom Robert had recommended so highly! He might be clean shaven and young but he was not weak. He was humble, but he was strong. Suddenly Edward Hare loved him, and he said, "There are plenty of giants to slay here in New Zealand, too, John. We need young people like you who keep close to God. And you can depend on me to help you in every way that I can."

And Edward Hare did help John Fulton in every way that he could. He introduced him to the prominent people in Auckland. He took him around to visit the members of the church, and to his astonishment he found that John Fulton *could* preach and that the people came to hear him gladly. He helped John advertise his series of meetings, and as the months went by he rejoiced to see the church membership grow under John's ministry.

Toward the end of the following year, 1895, a letter came from the General Conference that threatened to shatter the happiness of several good people in Auckland.

"Dear Elder Fulton," the letter read, "Elder J. M. Cole has been laboring in Fiji for about a year now. He has made a good beginning, but ill health threatens to cut short his term of service. So we are recommending that as soon as possible you and your family proceed to Suva, Fiji, to join Elder Cole in the work in this needy field."

"Fiji!" gasped Susie. "Fiji! We are to work with John and Fanny Cole? Oh, John, how wonderful!" And she threw her arms around John and cried for joy.

John went at once to give Edward Hare the news. But Edward Hare was not pleased. "Fiji?" he scowled. "No! No! John, not Fiji! We need you here in New Zealand. God is blessing your work here in Auckland and there are many other large towns that must be worked."

"But, Brother Edward, I have always wanted to be a missionary ever since I was a little boy, and I believe God is calling me to Fiji."

"Missionary? Yes, John, and you can be a missionary right here in New Zealand. But Fiji! John, don't you know that those islands used to be called the Cannibal Islands?"

"Yes, but——"

"Now, listen, John, I've got a little book here," and Edward went over to his bookshelf, picked it out and handed it to John. "It is called *From Dark to Dawn in Fiji*, by R. Vernon. It was published just three or four years ago in London. If ever you wanted your hair to stand on end, all you'd need to do is to read this book. I tell you it horrified me. No missionaries ever had a more degraded people to work for than the Wesleyan missionaries William Cross and David Cargill who landed in Lakemba from Tonga in 1835. They found the Fijians had a reckless disregard for human life. They not only killed and ate their enemies of war, they regarded *mbokola* [human flesh] as a delicacy. For a feast the chiefs would seize someone against whom they had ill will, together with their wives and even their children. Then they would cut them up, cook them in their underground hot-stone ovens and eat them. They said *mbokola* tasted like pork, and the human bodies being prepared for cooking were called *vuaka mbalavu* ["long pig"]."

"Yes, but——" John tried to interrupt.

"Yes, but that's not half," went on Edward Hare. "You can't imagine the cruelty of those people. It was common for old people, when they became helpless or sick, to be strangled or buried alive. They tell of one young woman who was delicate and quite sick for some time. The chief's son decided to put an end to her weakness. So he ordered a grave to be dug just outside of her house. Then the young woman was seized and thrown in. 'Don't bury me,' she cried, 'I am quite well now!' But strong hands held her down while the dirt was thrown in on her till her cries were heard no more. The story is right there in that book.

"Jealous wives of a chief were known to cut off or bite off the noses of the other wives they hated, and a very common sign of sorrow at the loss of a loved one was to cut off a joint of the little finger, and another joint and still another for each succeeding loss.

"When a chief was ready to launch a new war canoe, he seized twenty or thirty of his poor people, and tying their hands and legs together, used their live bodies as rollers over which the heavy war canoe was launched. If they lived through the ordeal —fine. But many of them had their lives crushed out in this way."

"Yes, but——" John tried to interrupt again.

But Edward Hare wasn't ready for any interruption yet, and lifting his hand for silence, he went on:

"Yes, and when a chief died, his wives, his servants, and even his mother if she was still living, were all strangled. They

Monument to the first missionaries to arrive in the Fiji Islands. The inscription reads:

"Cross and Cargill
First Missionaries
Arrived
14th Oct, 1835"

became 'grass' for lining the chief's grave. They were laid on a
layer of mats in the bottom of the grave and then the chief was
laid on top of them! And the surprising thing about it is that
the custom was so strong that the women and servants regarded
it as an honor to be buried with the chief. When the early missionaries tried to save them the poor benighted people insisted
on being strangled! And that's not all. When a chief built a
new house, wide post holes eight feet deep were dug in the
ground. The posts were then put in, and a man was put in with
the post to hold it upright, then the dirt was filled in and the
man was buried alive."

Edward Hare paused for breath and shuddered with the
horror of his tale. John seized the opportunity and broke in,
"Yes, but, Brother Edward, that was sixty years ago! Since
then the Fijians have become Christians."

"Well," admitted Edward Hare, "that may have been sixty
years ago, but don't think for a moment that the Fijians became
Christians overnight. There is a simple monument in the heart
of Suva today erected to the memory of Cross and Cargill, and
if ever human beings earned a monument, they certainly did.
They were befriended by a few, hated and persecuted by others;
their lives were often in danger, and they were often overwhelmed with discouragement. But little by little they did lay
the foundation for Christianity, and began the translation of the
New Testament. Four years later, so it says in that book, in De-
cember, 1838, they were joined by two more Methodist missionary families from England, James Calvert and his wife,
and John Hunt and his wife. Hunt established a mission on the
island of Viwa, off the east coast of Viti Levu, the largest of the
Fijian islands, and close to Mbau, a tiny island where the
paramount chief, or the Fijian king, had his headquarters.
Calvert continued on at Lakemba for a number of years. Both
families endured hardships beyond description, but they suc-

ceeded in completing the Fijian New Testament by 1847, just thirteen years after the arrival of the first missionaries. The Old Testament was completed a few years later and, look there! I've got a marker at page 112. It tells how Thakombau the cannibal king was converted and baptized in 1857, just twenty-three years after the arrival of the first missionaries!"

"Wonderful! Wonderful!" ejaculated John, as he opened the book and glanced at the page.

"Yes, it was wonderful all right," continued Edward, "and that was just thirty-eight years ago. And they say that today you can go to Mbau and still see old Thakombau's council house where twenty-one Tongans were buried alive in the post holes, and if you go into the Methodist church there, right in front of the pulpit you will see a great stone. It is now used as a baptismal font for sprinkling converts. Well, that stone was the very stone against which old King Thakombau ordered his victims' heads to be smashed before they were cooked and eaten."

"So then it is quite safe for anybody to go to Fiji now," said John Fulton eagerly.

"Wait a minute," said Edward Hare, "that was not the end of cannibalism. Listen! Just twenty-eight years ago, in 1867, Mr. Baker, a Wesleyan missionary, and a band of Fijian assistants traveled up the Wainimbuka River to the mountainous district of Tholo in the interior of Viti Levu, the largest of the Fijian islands. They entered the village of Numbutautau where old Chief Wawambalavu lived. At first they were well received and it looked as if the old chief was about to have his men sound the *lali* [wooden drum made of a hollowed-out log] to call the people together for a preaching service. But unfortunately there was a man in that village who had a grudge against Mr. Baker. He called the chief outside and holding up a whale's tooth, which the Fijians touch when they make solemn oaths, he tried to get the chief to promise to kill Mr. Baker. But the chief wouldn't do it, and went inside again. As he continued to talk with Mr. Baker, the chief noticed a comb in Mr. Baker's pocket and asked to borrow it. The chief combed his hair with it for a while, then left it stuck in his hair. Now there were two things that either Mr. Baker didn't know or that he forgot. One was never to ask a chief to return anything, and the other was never to touch a chief's hair. Anyway, Mr. Baker asked to get his comb back, and when the chief took no notice of his request, he playfully reached over and took the comb from the chief's hair, and that did it. At once the chief got up and went out, found the man who had the grudge against Mr. Baker, touched the whale's tooth, and made an oath to kill the missionary. Mr. Baker and his companions spent the night in the chief's house, but they knew there was something the matter. 'We had better get away from here quickly,' the Fijian companions said to Mr. Baker. 'The chief seems angry.' 'Yes, I'm afraid I offended him by taking back my comb,' said Mr. Baker. 'We will leave first thing in the morning.'

"As they were leaving, the chief offered to go with them a little way, and when they were out on a nearby hillside, he called to his men to close in on Mr. Baker and club him to death. The Fijian assistants were able to escape, but Mr. Baker's body was dragged to a precipice, over which it was thrown onto a path many feet below. The body was then dragged several miles upriver to a big flat rock that looked like a table. There it was cut up, washed, cooked in a hot-stone oven, and eaten at old Chief Wawambalavu's feast!"

Edward Hare paused a moment for the shocking story to sink in a little, then went on. "John, the cannibals cooked and ate Mr. Baker just twenty-eight years ago! Now do you still want to go to Fiji? Don't you think you had better stay here in New Zealand where you are needed, and where there is no fear of your being cooked and eaten?"

"Brother Edward," replied John, "I have had a desire to be a missionary to the Pacific Islands ever since I was five years old, when my mother used to tell me stories about John Williams and John Geddie and the Gordons in the New Hebrides, and I feel that God is calling me to Fiji. Things just can't be as bad *today* as you describe. Hasn't the British Government stopped cannibalism?"

"Oh, yes! You see when old King Thakombau became a Christian, he realized that no Fijian king could ever bring peace to the many chiefs who were so jealous of one another that they were continually fighting and killing one another's people, so in October, 1874, as you can see in that book, he ceded the Fiji Islands to Queen Victoria of Great Britain and sent his old favorite war club to her as a present. Since that time the British have been in charge, and since about 1890 cannibalism has not been heard of."

"Aren't the majority of the Fijians at least nominal Christians today?" broke in John.

"Well, yes. Methodists and Roman Catholics," admitted Edward a bit reluctantly. "But I tell you, John, there are a lot of them still in league with the old devil himself. Listen to this. On the rocky shore of the island of Kandavu, there are two large roundish rocks. At certain times the women from a nearby village dress up in their best clothes, clamber up on those rocks, and chant a request for a huge turtle they have named Raunindalithe to come to the surface and show itself. Believe it or not, after chanting this request two or three times, up comes this great turtle, pokes his head above the water as if to say, 'Here I am, ladies,' then after a while down he goes again. After resting a moment the women chant for Tinandi Thambonga [Mother of Turtles] to appear, and believe it or not in a minute or two up comes the mother of turtles, half as big again as the first monster. She floats on the surface for a minute then slowly sinks

John I. Tay's grave. Standing on the left, R. L. Aveling; on the right,
Agnes Fulton Hare.

down into the depths again! Now, John Fulton, if that isn't being in league with the devil, what is it? No white man has ever been able to fathom their secret."

"Is that so?" said John in amazement.

"Yes it is," replied Edward emphatically. "And here's one to beat that. On the little island of Mbengga there is a group of people called fire walkers. They dig a pit two or three feet deep and fill it with big stones. Then they pile firewood on top of the pit, set the wood on fire and keep it burning for twenty-four hours. During the night preceding the ceremony the fire walkers stay together in a nearby hut. If you ask them what they do all night, they will say, 'We talk with a small devil.' Apparently this is so, for the next morning, after the embers are raked off and the red-hot stones are smoothed out, they come out of the hut looking as if they were in a trance. They walk in single file and slowly circle around on the stones. When they are finished their assistants throw damp leaves on the rocks, and the hissing clouds of steam prove how hot the stones are, and yet no one has ever discovered a burn or a blister on the feet of those fire walkers! White men have looked again and again for some evidence of trickery but have found none! I tell you, John, they are in league with the devil himself."

John waited a moment at the close of this story, then said, "The greater the darkness, Brother Edward, the greater the need of the light of the gospel! Susie and I must go to Fiji."

"Yes, I suppose you will go. That's just the way John I. Tay and his wife talked, and how long did he live? He saw the need. He threw himself into the work, but his body was not made for all the sickness and disease of those islands, and in five months he got sick and died. And now John Cole and his wife are there and they are sick. Who can tell whether they will ever get out alive? And now you and Susie want to go and take your two darling little girls! John, have you no heart? Don't you love your wife and children? Then why don't you stay here in New Zealand where you are loved and needed?"

For a moment John was silent. Then he rose, took Edward by the hand, and said "Thank you, Brother Edward, for what you have told me. Thank you for your words of warning. Thank you for wanting me to stay right here. But none of these things move me, neither do I count my life dear to myself. As the Lord Jesus counted the cost, then came into this world to save me, so I have counted the cost and am willing to take the gospel light to those who sit in darkness. Susie and I and our two little girls will go to Fiji."

Edward Hare listened intently to what John said. It was hard to tell by the half smile that lighted up his face whether he really approved or was just satisfied. Then he said, "John, of course you will go to Fiji, and God will go with you. Already your words sound like the words of a decided Fijian. You know they are notorious for being hard to move. When they were cannibals, they were consistently cannibals, and when they become Christians they are just as consistent and are not to be moved. John, I am proud of you. I pay tribute to your consistency. You are a decided, immovable Fijian missionary, John. God bless you."

Misi Fulitoni

THE NEWS SPREAD around to all the church members like wildfire, and there were quite a number who felt just as Edward Hare did.

"The Fultons! Going to Fiji! With those two darling little girls! Whatever will they do if they get sick? And what kind of school will they find for them?" Back and forth they asked these questions and discussed the problems that would surely befall the Fultons if they should go to such a primitive place. But finally, seeing John and Susie had made up their minds and would not be changed, they accepted it as inevitable.

"Of course," wrote Pastor Daniells in reply to John Fulton's letter telling him about his appointment to Fiji, "we will want you to attend the camp meeting in Auckland before you go."

"I'll be glad to," John wrote back. And he did attend. John and Susie stayed in a tent on the campground, and almost next door to them the Guiliard family from Napier had their tent. There were Father Guiliard and Mother Guiliard, a son, Bert, a daughter, Edith, who was fourteen going on fifteen, and another daughter, Maud, a few years younger. The news of the Fultons' approaching departure for Fiji created quite a stir. Edith spent a lot of time with four-year-old Jessie and two-

61

The Fultons just before they left for Fiji.

and-a-half-year-old Agnes. She looked with awe upon Susie
Fulton. "You're going to be real missionaries in Fiji," she gasped.
"How wonderful!"

Mrs. Guiliard and Susie became well acquainted during the
camp meeting also. "We wish you could come and spend a
week with us at Napier before you go," she begged.

"Maybe we can," replied Susie. And sure enough things
worked out that way. The little church in Napier was thrilled
to have the young American missionary-to-be with them for
the weekend. But for Edith it was a different matter. "Oh,
Mother, I dont want to see them go," she cried. "I've just
fallen in love with Jessie and Agnes, and I will miss them so
much." And in spite of her almost fifteen years, she put her
head on her mother's shoulder and wept.

"There, there now. Don't cry," comforted her mother.
"You'll get over it, my dear. The sun will still be shining tomorrow."

In spite of her mother's comfort, Edith lay awake a large
part of that night, and thought and thought and thought. In
the morning she had made up her mind. She dressed quickly,
tiptoed to the Fultons' room, and knocked on the door. "Mrs.
Fulton," she whispered, "what do you think I have decided
to do?"

"I have no idea," replied Susie Fulton smiling.

"I am going to Fiji with you!"

"But, Edith, how could you?"

"I've thought it all through. You will need someone to look
after Jessie and Agnes, and to teach them, and Elder Cole in
Suva has a little girl, Ruita, about as old as Agnes, and I have
finished grammar school, so I can be the teacher for the missionaries' children."

"But, Edith! Your parents! Have you asked them about this
wild idea of yours?"

"Not yet, but I will."

"Yes, but we couldn't pay you any wages, and the General Conference couldn't pay you!"

"But I could just be one of the family, couldn't I?" broke in Edith, and the look she gave Susie Fulton just melted her heart. "I could help with the housework while you helped Mr. Fulton give Bible studies. And if you got sick, I could help!"

"But your schooling, Edith?"

"Oh, well, in a few years maybe I could go to Avondale College in Australia. But for now, please, Mrs. Fulton, can't I go to Fiji with you and be one of your family? I think you need a big daughter like me, and I think Jessie and Agnes need a big sister like me. May I? Please, Mrs. Fulton?"

Susie Fulton was lost in thought for a few moments. She had learned to love this dear girl and her family. Maybe this wild idea of hers did have some good sense in it. She put her arm tenderly about this would-be big daughter and said, "Well, Edith, I'll talk with Mr. Fulton about it, and we will pray about it and see what your parents think about it, and then we will decide."

"Oh, thank you, Mrs. Fulton. Thank you!" cried Edith and she gave Susie Fulton a big hug. "I just know it will work out all right. I am sure it will." And it did. Of course, Edith's wild idea really shocked the Guiliard family for a few hours, but little by little father and mother's emphatic "No" softened to a "Maybe," and before long to a fond, "Well, all right, Edith, you can go for a year or two."

And so it came to pass that one fine day in May, 1896, John and Susie Fulton with four-year-old Jessie, two-and-a-half-year-old Agnes, and their new big daughter, nearly fifteen-year-old Edith Guiliard, got on the boat, waved good-by to friends and loved ones in Auckland, and steamed northward across the South Pacific Ocean toward Fiji, their mission field.

After a very rough one-thousand-mile voyage, which took about five days, their boat steamed into the calm waters of Suva harbor. It anchored for an hour or so some distance from the wharf while the doctors from the health department, the customs officials, and the police came on board and began their inspection. The members of the Fulton family were all up on deck, fascinated by the native boats, canoes, and sailing craft that swarmed around them. They were manned by stalwart looking men dressed in *sulus* (cloths from waist to knees) and sweat shirts, and every one had a well-trimmed bushy head of hair.

"Susie!" whispered John.

"Yes, John?"

"There they are, our Fijians!"

"Yes, John. Our Fijians."

"I wonder if any of those boatmen are Christians? Or are any of them still in league with the devil?"

"I wonder too."

There was a pause in their conversation for a moment or two, then John went on, "Susie, at last here we are in the mission field. I can't describe the desire I have in my heart to save some of these dear people and to bring to them the precious light of the third angel's message."

"I too have the same desire, John."

"Susie, come down to the cabin with me for a little while," whispered John. "I want us to dedicate our hearts to God for this solemn work."

Susie nodded and together they went to their cabin. When they came back on deck their faces shone with their consecration.

At last the doctors were satisfied that there was no communicable sickness on board the boat. The quarantine flag was pulled down, and the steamer moved slowly nearer and nearer

5

Mr. and Mrs. John M. Cole

to the wharf. The Fultons gazed intently at the waving crowd, trying to pick out the Coles. They were looking for a man who wasn't smoking, with a wife, and a little——

"There they are!" shouted Edith. "Look over there by the customs house door! It must be! They are the only ones with a little girl as small as Agnes."

All eyes turned in that direction. "Yes! It is! It is!" cried Susie. "There is Fanny, and there is John, and that little girl must be Ruita!" And they waved and shouted frantically. The Coles waved back and shouted, "Welcome to Fiji!"

The process of disembarking and going through customs was exciting, and then came the greetings. The two Johns shook hands and slapped each other on the back as they said, "At last we are real missionaries! In a real mission field!" Susie and Fanny hugged and kissed each other and murmured their great joy at being together again. Jessie and Agnes looked shyly at Ruita, while Edith introduced herself to them and said, "Ruita, I'm going to be your teacher."

Now add to all this excitement the Fijian tropical heat and you will understand why they were quite exhausted after they and their baggage had arrived at Brother Cole's home in the town of Suva. "Well, John," said John Cole as Fanny was passing around some cool drinks, "one of the first things we have to do is to find a place for you to live."

"And I suppose that will not be too easy," suggested John Fulton.

"Well, that all depends. Last year there was a hurricane that blew down several houses at Tamavua, a village about two miles from here. One of those houses, near a big mango tree, now looks like a big pile of rubbish. But it is for sale, and I can see possibilities in it. Would you like to go and look at it?"

"Indeed I would. It sounds interesting to me," said John.

"I thought it would," said John Cole. "But before we go to see the owner let me tell you what your new names are going to be."

"New names?" questioned the Fultons. "Are we to have new names before we get to heaven?"

"Yes, new names. You see, the Fijians do not use any final consonants in their language, so every syllable of our names that ends in a consonant must have a vowel added to it, which means another syllable also, so your name 'Fulton,' will be Fulitoni [Fu-li-to-ne]. For Mister, they say Misi [mi-se]. So John, you will be Misi Fulitoni. But quite often they will just call you *Turanga* which means "master." Mrs. Fulton will be Marama Fulitoni. There will be no change for Jessie. They can say that name quite well, but Agnes will be called Aganisi [A-ga-ne-se]."

"Then you are Misi Coli [Co-le], John, eh?"

"Exactly! You're learning quickly!" replied John Cole. "You are going to enjoy learning to speak Fijian, John. They use our Roman letters, but some of the letters have a different sound. For example, C is pronounced *th*. There is a distinct *m* sound before *b* making it *mb,* and an *n* sound before *d* and *g* making those two letters sound *nd* and *ng*."

"Oh! I must remember that," said John.

"Now you see why we pronounce the name of the last Fijian cannibal king, written Cakobau, 'Tha-kom-bau.' "

"I see. And of course I've heard of him."

"Now, listen while I tell you the name of our church. It is not easy to say Seventh-day Adventist Church in Fijian. The words have to be explained a little, so they say, *Na lotu sa vakambauta talenga na nona lako tali mai na Turanga*. This means, 'The church which believes in the Sabbath and believes in the second coming of the Lord.' "

"Oh dear! That's too long for a name."

The old mango tree near the place where the Fultons' first house was built.

Government offices at Suva on Viti Levu.

"Yes, that's what they all said, so they shortened it to *Na lotu ni kavitu ni singa,* 'The church of the seventh day.'"

"That's better!" agreed Misi Fulitoni.

"But there's another name still shorter by which we are nearly always called. It didn't take the Fijians long to see how different we were from the other Christian churches here. We didn't smoke or drink liquor, or even drink tea or coffee, or eat unclean meats or fish, so they began to refer to us as *Na Lotu Savasava,* 'The Clean Church.' And, John, that name has stuck, and we are known as *Na Lotu Savasava* everywhere we go."

Fortunately, Misi Fulitoni had saved enough money to buy the lot with the big mango tree and the pile of rubbish on it, and as the days went by the Fulitoni house began to take shape with the help of some interested friends. As it turned out, the pile of rubbish contained enough lumber to build two houses. So John Cole decided to build a house for himself right beside John Fulton's house.

As the two missionaries worked together, John Cole had time to recount his experiences in Fiji up to the present time. "John," he said, "when we first came here we didn't know where to go or where to begin. We were told that there were maybe two hundred and fifty islands altogether in the group, with eighty of them inhabited. There were less than half a million people altogether made up of Fijians and Indians from India. Viti Levu where we are now living is the largest island, but the capital was then at Levuka on the small island of Ovalau, a little distance to the east, so we went there."

"And you didn't stay there?"

"No, we soon found that Suva was the most important port, and the government was building in Suva and planning to move there as soon as possible, so we came here, and we feel that God's providence led us to this place."

"Good! And how long was it before you could preach and hold meetings?"

"Well, of course I didn't wait till I could speak Fijian before I started to hold meetings, John. I visited around among those who could speak English, and soon found a fellow who had been in America and who could speak English and Fijian fluently. He wasn't much of a Christian and he drank quite a little liquor, but hoping for the best, I hired him as a teacher to teach me Fijian and to translate for me. Then I started right in holding meetings. For a few months my translator felt challenged to be on his best behavior and we were pleased to see the interest growing and the attendance at our meetings increasing. But this fellow was not at all interested in salvation; he was interested only in his money, and when the newness of his work wore off, he again gave himself up to liquor, and many times he was so drunk that I couldn't be sure of what he was saying. John, it was like trying to preach the gospel through a beer barrel, so I had to let him go."

"And now?"

"Well, John, I find more than enough to keep me busy in working for those who speak English. I'm not too fluent in Fijian, but you are younger than I am. The language will come easier for you. You will be preaching fluently in Fijian within a year. You'll see! I only hope that your health will stand up better than mine. I have trouble with my stomach. Fanny says I work too hard and worry too much about the work. But whatever it is, there are times when I can't eat anything but soup or gruel, and even then I have much pain and distress."

"Maybe ulcers, eh?"

"Maybe."

So the two men worked and talked till their homes were completed sometime in August and their families moved in.

"You must come and inspect our palace, Fanny," said Susie.

"We are as happy and as comfortable as a king and a queen."
As Fanny came in, Susie proudly took her from room to room
and pointed to her furniture. "See that magnificent table,
Fanny? It's just two big box lids that John fixed together and
put on legs! See those beautifully draped cupboards? Well,
they are old packing boxes that we brought with us from New
Zealand, with dainty curtains around them! And these seats?
More draped boxes."

Fanny smiled her approval. "You're real missionaries all
right!" she said.

"Of course, we bought the beds, but we made the mattresses.
I sewed up some just-the-right-size sacks, and John filled them
with straw! Fortunately, John is a good handyman! So we will
manage till we can afford to buy something better."

"That's exactly what we did, both on Norfolk Island and
here," Fanny confided. And with real admiration she said, "I
am proud of you, Susie."

Susie was quiet for a moment then said, "Fanny, could I
ask you something personal?"

"Sure."

"Fanny, we haven't had our wages for July or August from
the General Conference yet. Have you had yours?"

"No, we haven't," replied Fanny. "But don't worry, Susie.
The two big stores in Suva will let us charge our groceries, and
our money is sure to come from the General Conference someday soon."

They were able to charge their groceries that month all
right. But in September, still no money came. However, a letter
came. It explained that the General Conference funds were so
low they couldn't send any money yet, but they would send
their wages as soon as possible.

Nevertheless that month something did come. Can you
imagine what it was? It was the missionary ship *Pitcairn* on its

fifth trip around our Pacific Island missions, and it brought a
good supply of dried prunes and beans for the faithful missionary families in Fiji.

"Now we will have beans to help change the monotony of
yams and taro, and yams and taro," said Susie to Fanny.

"Yes, but poor John," said Fanny. "Beans are hard on his
poor stomach."

"You know," confessed Susie, "I suppose if we had been
brought up on this native food it would be different. When we
first began to use coconut milk instead of cow's milk, which
we could not afford, we thought it was delicious. But whether
it is too rich or whether it is just the monotony of it I don't
know, but I find myself just longing for some cow's milk."

"Or a can of peaches!" added Fanny.

"Or some real butter!"

"Sh-h-h," demanded Fanny. "Be thankful you now have
beans and prunes."

"I am thankful," insisted Susie. "So thankful." Then her
face flushed a little as she whispered, "Fanny, there's something
I've been wanting to tell you."

"Oh?"

"Fanny, I've got a secret."

"You have? Will you give me three guesses?"

"Fanny, you don't need three guesses."

"Oh, Susie, I'm so glad for you. There's nothing like a new
baby in the family to take your mind off of all your miseries."

"Or the monotony of yams, taro, and beans!" added Susie
with a smile.

"And when are you expecting its arrival?"

"Sometime around my birthday, April 4."

"Wonderful, Susie. And you can count on me to help in
any way that I can."

Another month went slowly by. The two missionary men

spent their time studying the language and preaching in the nearby villages. Usually they preached in the open air while the people sat on the grass around them. But quite often, especially on Sundays, they were invited to preach in the little Wesleyan churches that were found nearly everywhere. Misi Coli did the preaching when there was no interpreter available, and Misi Fulitoni listened and quickly learned to speak Fijian. They were always careful to preach on the prophecies that foretold the second coming of Christ in a way that would not give any offense.

Susie and Fanny made friends with the village women. They showed the women how to sew little dresses and little pants and shirts for their children, and the women in turn showed them how to prepare taro greens with coconut milk, and how to fix yams and breadfruit in several ways to break the monotony of their diet. And, of course, as they exchanged these helpful ideas, the missionary ladies soon learned to speak Fijian.

Meanwhile Edith and her little group of missionary children, Jessie, Agnes, and Ruita, were doing missionary service of their own kind with the nearby village children. Jessie, of course, had to spend some time at reading, writing, and arithmetic, but a large portion of the day was spent playing hide-and-seek and tag among the mango trees and the banana trees with the village children. As you may imagine, one of their favorite games was playing Sabbath school. Edith would lead out singing songs and telling Bible stories. It was only a game, but it is impossible to tell whether the village children learned more English than the missionary children learned Fijian. At any rate the missionary children were talking simple Fijian in just a few months, and the village children loved playing Sabbath school so much that they came to the real Sabbath school on Sabbaths.

At the end of October, again no money came from the General Conference. "This makes four months without money," sighed Fanny as she visited one day with Susie. "We have never been left as long as this before."

"Fanny, we must remember that there are only about fifty thousand Seventh-day Adventists in all the world," Susie tried to explain, "and the need for missionaries is greater than they can readily fill. Just last year they sent D. A. Robinson to open up work in India, and the year before that they sent F. H. Westphal to open up work in South America. So I suppose the General Conference is finding it hard to have enough money to send around to everyone."

"Maybe that's it," agreed Fanny. "Our turn is sure to come. But it is getting so embarrassing to get groceries at the store and say, 'Charge it.'" Fanny was quiet for a moment, then she whispered, "Susie, there's something I've been wanting to tell you."

"Yes?" said Susie with a twinkle in her eye.

"Susie, I've got a secret."

"You have? Will you give me three guesses?"

"Susie, you don't need three guesses."

"Oh, Fanny, I'm so glad for you. There's nothing like a new baby to take one's mind off of the embarrassment of saying, 'Charge it' at the store. And when are *you* expecting your little one's arrival?"

"Somewhere around *my* birthday, May the tenth."

"Wonderful! Wonderful!" exclaimed Susie. "And, Fanny, you can count on me to help in any way that I can."

"Thank you, thank you, Susie dear. I know you will," said Fanny, "and I just can't find words to tell you how happy John and I are that Misi Fulitoni and Marama Fulitoni are with us here in Fiji."

The Fulton home at Suva Vou.

A typical Fijian village.

Tested and Tried

AS THE MONTH OF NOVEMBER, 1896, began to unfold, little Aganisi's eyes began to sparkle. "How many more sleeps till my birthday, Mamma?" she asked every morning.

"Only a few more sleeps," answered her mother. "You'll be three years old on the ninth."

"Will I be a big girl then, Mamma?"

"Of course."

"And will I have a party?"

"Well, I hope——"

"And a cake?"

"I do hope——"

"And some presents?"

"Oh, Aganisi, how I wish I could say Yes. A party with a cake and some presents. But, Aganisi, we have no money."

"Will it come someday, Mamma?"

"Of course. And if it comes before your birthday, we'll have the party and the cake and the presents and everything. But if——"

"And if it doesn't come, we could have the party and the cake and the presents *after* the money comes. Couldn't we, Mamma?"

"Of course, my darling."

The money didn't come in time for the birthday. It didn't come by the end of the month. "But it's sure to come before Christmas, isn't it, Mother?" asked Jessie, looking very serious as she tried her hand at dispensing a little comfort.

"Oh, I do hope it will" replied mother.

"Of course it's sure to come before Christmas," put in Edith, also trying to sound as hopeful and be as helpful as she possibly could.

But the money didn't come before Christmas, and it didn't come before New Year's.

Time and time again John reverently took out the copy of Sister White's letter to Uncle Samuel, and read, "The cloud may appear dark to you at times in itself, but when filled with the bright light of Jesus, it is turned to the brightness of gold, for the glory of God is upon it." He read those precious, comforting words over and over to Susie, and their courage was renewed and their faith sustained. He read those precious, comforting words to John Cole and his good wife, Fanny, and they both took courage. But he was just human enough to add, "Six months without any money, John! Do you suppose the General Conference has forgotten us?"

"No, sir! I don't believe the General Conference has forgotten us," John Cole replied.

"Well, we surely have prayed enough about it. Maybe the Lord has forgotten us?"

"No, sir, John! The Lord has not forgotten us! But do you know what I believe?"

"What?"

"I believe the Lord is permitting this to happen as a test! You remember Adam was tested and tried on three points: His fleshly desires—appetite; his faith in God—Hath God really said? and, his ambition and pride—Ye shall be as gods."

"That's right," agreed John Fulton.

"And when Jesus was about to begin His ministry, *He* was tested and tried on those same three points: Fleshly desires— appetite—Make these stones bread; Faith in God—Cast your- self down, for His angels will protect you; and, His pride and ambition—Worship me just once and I will give you all the kingdoms of the world."

"That's right!"

"Yes, it is right," said John Cole. "And, John, the Lord is testing and trying us now. Before He can trust us with success He must be sure that we are not mere hirelings, working for the bread we eat. He must be sure that we will believe in Him no matter what happens, and He must be sure that no worldly ambition can lure us from our duty to Him."

"That's right! God *proved* the children of Israel, too, at the bitter waters of Marah."

"Yes, and remember James says, 'Blessed is the man that *endureth* temptation: for when he is tried, he shall receive the crown of life, which the Lord hath promised to them that love him' (James 1:12)."

"Yes, and Job said, 'He knoweth the way that I take: when he hath tried me, I shall come forth as gold' (Job 23:10). Yes, John, I believe it. It is clear that God is just testing and trying us. I know we are safe in the hands of God no matter what happens."

The two men were quiet for a moment as they thought and renewed their consecration to God, then John Cole went on, "And say, John, we have another problem coming up. Not only have we been without money for six months, not only do we find ourselves inwardly weary of the monotony of our food and longing for the milk and honey and the peaches and cream of our homeland, but do you know it hasn't rained for several weeks and the water in our tanks is almost gone? We have had to limit its use for just cooking and drinking. If it doesn't rain soon, I don't know what we will do."

"There is a little stream at the foot of our hill that empties into the bay."

"But the tide rising and falling each day makes its water so brackish that it is not usable."

"I wonder how far up the ravine we would have to go before we found the water fresh enough for us to use?"

"Why don't we go for a walk sometime and find out?"

"All right! Come on, let us go now!" agreed John Fulton. So the two Johns went down the hill to the little stream and began walking up the ravine. The dense tropical undergrowth made their walking difficult. But they hadn't gone far before John Fulton stopped short and said, "Listen! What's that sound I hear?"

John Cole stopped, cocked his head in the direction of the sound, and held his breath. And then he heard it too, clear and distinct. "It sounds like falling water to me!"

"A spring?"

"It could be! Let us go home and get our chopping knives and cut our way to that sound and see!"

"Let's do that," said John Fulton excitedly, and they did. They got their big knives and cut their way to the sound, and found a beautiful spring and a pool of sweet fresh water.

"We've found a spring of water nearby!" they shouted to their Fijian neighbors.

"Impossible!" they cried. "We've lived here all our lives and never heard of a spring of water anywhere near here."

"Well, come and see!"

They went and saw, and were amazed. *"Sombo! Sombo!"* they cried. "Where did this spring of water come from?"

In their hearts the two missionaries believed that their God had either provided the spring of water or had led them to discover it just when they needed it, to assure them that He was still with them and would never leave them nor forsake them (Heb. 13:5). So they thanked God and took courage.

January came and went, but no money came. February came and went and still no money came. But money or no money, John Fulton and John Cole continued their visiting and preaching in the surrounding villages.

The town of Suva was in the center of a large semicircular bay, which was protected by a coral reef that acted as an excellent breakwater. About two miles across the bay from Suva, near the southwest end of the bay, there was a village called Suva Vou (New Suva). In that village there lived an old chief by the name of Ratu Ambrose. The chief was a nominal Christian, and had built the Wesleyan church there. Whenever John Cole and John Fulton came to Suva Vou the chief always attended their meetings, and if they happened to come on a Sunday he invited Misi Coli to preach in his church.

"You had better look out for Ratu Ambrose," confided John Cole one day as they were coming back home across the bay in a small boat from a meeting at Suva Vou.

"Yes?" questioned John Fulton.

"Yes! and I mean yes!" declared John Cole vehemently. "That man is a descendant of the old cannibal king Thakombau. Here in his district they call him King of Suva and, John, if the old Fijian Government were in power today, he *would* be king of Fiji. But that man is not honest. He once held a high government office, but they say he embezzled funds and was guilty of sedition. Anyway, he was banished for some time, and has been in prison several times because of his evil deeds."

"He seems sincere enough now," broke in John Fulton.

"Maybe he *looks* it. But several of the government men have warned me about him. 'Look out for old Ratu Ambrose!' they cautioned. 'He will do anything for money! And if he thinks

6

there is any money in it he would even become a Seventh-day Adventist.' "

"Dear me! He doesn't look that bad to me," again broke in John Fulton.

"Well, you ought to ask his wife, Andi Kilara [Queen Clara], then. She could tell you. He learned to love the Englishman's whisky, and when he gets drunk he beats poor Kilara half to death and pulls her clothes off. She has often had to flee half-naked to save her life."

"Dear me! What a man!"

"What a man, is right! He himself boasts that there is no sin he has not committed, and everybody knows that he cheated the Wesleyan Mission out of a sum of money in such a clever way that they couldn't take him to court!"

"Dear me! Dear me!"

"So you see it's no wonder that everybody says, 'Look out for old Ratu Ambrose.' "

"No, it's no wonder," agreed John Fulton thoughtfully. Then he added, "But I wonder if he is too great a sinner for the dear Lord Jesus to save?"

They sailed on in silence for a while. Then John Fulton changed the subject. "John," he said thoughtfully, "here it is March and still no money from the General Conference! Nine months without money is a long time. My poor wife is finding it harder and harder to keep up her strength on only the native foods. What can we do? It is just too embarrassing to go to the store and say, 'Charge it,' when we have owed them money so long. And we can't expect the poor Indian milkmen to sell us milk on credit. How poor Susie longs for a drink of real cow's milk!"

"Fanny too," added John Cole.

"You know, it will be time to take Susie to the hospital any day now."

"Yes, and I do hope these months of privation won't affect the baby."

"I surely hope not," sighed John Fulton.

Susie's time came on April 3, and John took her to the hospital. "Yes, she's a bit pale and run down," said the doctor, "but we will hope for the best for both the baby and the mother. You can count on my doing my utmost for both of them."

John waited nervously during the longest hours he had ever lived. At last the doctor called him in and pointed to a little baby boy apparently lifeless, lying on the table. "I'm sorry, Mr. Fulton, but there's not much hope for the baby, and I'll have to work hard to save Mrs. Fulton's life," he said.

John seemed too stunned to comprehend, and just stood there for a moment. "This just can't be!" he murmured to himself. Then—was that a slight movement he saw in the baby's body? He picked it up, went into the next room, asked a Fijian nurse to bring some hot water. Then he placed the baby first in hot water, then in cold. He kept on repeating this treatment, and soon the baby began to breathe, and then to cry! The baby was alive!

With God's blessing Susie also pulled through. "Shall we call him George after my father?" asked John, when Susie had regained her strength.

"That's splendid," agreed Susie, "and let's call him Lorin for his second name. I don't know anyone else called Lorin, but I like the name." So they called him George Lorin Fulton. "He was almost a birthday present, wasn't he?" smiled Susie.

"Just one day early," John replied.

"There's just one other thing I would like for a birthday present," sighed Susie. "Can you guess what it is?"

"I think I can guess. Would it be a check from the General Conference?"

"Oh, John, how much longer can we wait?"

The days dragged on halfway through April—the tenth month without money. And then one day John met a man who said with some excitement, "Oh, Mr. Fulton, I was at the boat when the mail was unloaded and I saw a package with your name on it. It's at the post office now. Better go and see what it is."

John Fulton's heart beat fast. A package! Wouldn't Susie be surprised! Who could have sent it? He hastened his footsteps and was soon at the post office. "Yes, Mr. Fulton, there is a package for you," said the clerk as he put the package on the table. "And there's no customs duty to pay on it."

"Good," exclaimed John, and he meant it in more ways than one. "And there's no sender's name or address! Guess it is meant for a surprise." John took up the package, thanked the clerk, and hurried home as fast as he could go. He quickly told Susie the good news.

"Children!" called Susie. "A present from America! Come quickly and see what it is."

The children rushed into the house and crowded around while John removed the wrapping. Then suddenly all was stunned silence—the package contained *beans* and *prunes!*

"Beans!" moaned Susie. "If only it could have been a cow!"

"Or a doll," Aganisi put in.

But brave, courageous Susie recovered quickly and said, "Never mind, children, let us thank God for more beans and prunes." And they did. As they rose from their knees, Susie looked lovingly at the disappointed children and added, "Never mind, last month I wrote to Grandma Newlon in America and told her how hard up we are. And I'm sure we will get a nice present from her soon."

The month of May came and with it a steamer from America, but still no money! "Fanny," said Susie one day in a voice that could not hide her disappointment, "this is the eleventh month with no money. Don't you think the Lord has tested us enough?"

"Susie," Fanny bravely replied, "the Lord's ways are past finding out. But of one thing we can be sure. The Lord is still with us. Look at the way He helped our husbands find the spring! Look at the interest there is in the meetings that are being held! Look at your lovely little baby, Georgie! I hope my baby will be just as good and healthy when my birthday comes."

"Oh, it will be, Fanny. You certainly have had as good food as I had," comforted Susie.

"Yes, but my first baby, Ruita, was anemic and sickly, and I can't help worrying a little."

"I wonder how close it will come to your birthday?"

"My birthday is May 10. So we will soon know," replied Fanny.

And what do you know! On May the tenth John Cole took Fanny to the hospital, and the same day a lovely, fat, healthy, baby boy was born! "Let us call him Tavita," said Fanny. "That is Fijian for David. David was tested and tried more than we ever have been."

"All right," replied John Cole, "that's fine!" So they called the new baby Tavita and everybody in the mission family rejoiced. But their rejoicing did not last long. Just a day or two later John Cole became seriously ill. He couldn't keep anything on his stomach. The beans and the stress and strain had proved too much for him. His poor body just couldn't take it any longer. He had to go to bed.

John Fulton went to see him every day, and tried his best to comfort him and suggest something that might tempt his appetite. But all to no avail.

One day after his visit he said, "I'm going in to town today, Fanny. Is there anything I can do for you there?"

"Brother Fulton," said Fanny with some reluctance, "I wonder if you would mind trying to get me a box of oatmeal. Oatmeal gruel is the only thing John can keep in his stomach."

John Fulton didn't answer at once. It had been several months since they had last tried saying, "Charge it," at the two provision stores in town. The manager of one of the stores had been real nasty, and gave them to understand that he wanted the old account all paid up before they could charge anything more. The manager of the other store was kinder, but it was nevertheless embarrassing to say, "Charge it," when they had paid nothing for eleven months.

John Fulton stood there for a moment weighing the situation. He looked at his shoes, which he carried in his hands. The soles had long since worn through, and for several months he had been going barefoot around the house and in the villages. But for appearance sake he carried his shoes with him when he went to town and put them on before meeting with any English people. Then he looked at John, lying flat on his back. Tears came to his eyes, and he said softly, "I'll try, Fanny."

On his way to town he planned his strategy. He would arrive at the store of the kind manager at the noon hour, when only the clerk would be there. Then he would nonchalantly ask for a box of oatmeal, and simply say, "Charge it." Well, he got to the store at noon all right, but to his chagrin the clerks were all gone, and only the manager was there. There was nothing else that he could do. He just had to tell the manager the strait they were in. "I'm sure the money will come eventually," said John, "and we've tried not to charge up more than the bare necessities. But now John Cole is sick in bed. He must have some oatmeal. If you wouldn't mind charging it."

The manager's heart was touched. Tears glistened in his eyes. "I know you are honest men, Mr. Fulton," he said. "And I believe your money will come someday. Tell me, how much do you owe the other store?"

John told him the amount. The kind manager went to his cash till and said, "Mr. Fulton, I want you to take enough money to pay off that other store's account, and then I want you to walk around here and take all the groceries and supplies you can carry. And of course you can charge it."

"No, no, not the money!" said John. "The other man can wait for that as well as you can. But the groceries—I cannot thank you enough. May God bless you for it." John Fulton carried home two armloads of supplies and divided them between the two families.

May the twenty-fourth came. It was Jessie's fifth birthday. But they had no cake. They had no presents. I do not need to tell you why. You know why. The money had not come yet.

Then came the month of June and with it another steamer from America. Almost reluctantly John forced himself to go to the post office and ask for mail. The disappointment month after month had robbed him of the natural excitement that usually accompanies mail day. But this day there was a letter from the General Conference! And also a letter from Grandma Newlon. And another letter from the General Conference for John Cole! John's heart beat fast. He raced home. First he ran breathlessly to John Cole's house and gave him his letter. Then he rushed into his own home, shouting, "Susie, I think it's come at last! There's a letter from the General Conference, and a letter from Grandma Newlon too!"

Susie dropped what she was doing, excitedly called the children in, and then tremblingly opened Grandma Newlon's letter while John opened the letter from the General Conference.

"Is it good news, John?" asked Susie. But John couldn't speak. He just waved the check before them all and with a choked voice tried his best to say, "Eleven months' pay!"

Susie was not so choked up as John, and waving a ten-dollar bill before them all, said, "Good news! Good news! Grandma Newlon has sent us a cow!" The children clapped their hands, and danced up and down in delight.

"Now we can have my birthday party," cried Aganisi.

"And mine too!" said Jessie.

"And Georgie's too," put in mother.

"And Christmas too," added Edith.

"But first we will pay the tithe and our bills," said father, "and then we must get a pair of shoes for each of us!"

"And then we will buy a cow," said Susie, "and we will have all the real milk we want to drink."

"Goody! Goody!" shouted the children.

After many days of testing and trial, the days of plenty had come, and great was the joy thereof.

Over in the Coles's house there was great joy and rejoicing also. But although the stress and the strain were relieved, John Cole did not get better.

"I'm afraid, Mr. Cole, you will have to go back to America to get back your health," counseled the doctor.

"But I don't want to go and leave the Fultons here all alone," protested John.

"If you don't go, you will die," warned the doctor.

"I'd rather die than go back," John replied firmly.

"And then you'd be no good to the Fultons or to anybody," answered the doctor. "If you go back now, and regain your health, you may be able to come back again. You have many years of service ahead of you, if you are wise now."

The doctor's advice won out, and little by little John Cole became resigned to returning to America for a while. Letters from the General Conference agreed that this was the best thing to do, and he was invited to work in Oregon as soon as he was well enough.

Finally, in August, 1897, when little Tavita was just three

months old, the Coles sailed for America. The parting was
hard for both families, even though they all knew it was the
only thing to do. As they parted, John Cole said to John Fulton,
"You don't know how I hate to leave you. We are just getting
to the place where we can translate some tracts and hymns,
and then there is that group of good people almost ready for
baptism."

"Now don't worry about them, John," said John Fulton.
"I can talk enough Fijian now to ask questions and have them
read the answers from the Scriptures. And I'm sure that with
God's help I will be able to get them ready for baptism."

"I know you will," replied John Cole. "And I'll tell you
what! I'll never rest until with God's help I have bought you
a little printing press and have persuaded the General Conference to send another missionary couple to help you."

Alipati and Ratu Ambrose at the Australasian Union Conference in 1910.

Ratu Ambrose

GOD DID INDEED bless both of the men. Although John Fulton had been in Fiji only a little more than a year, he entered heartily into the giving of Bible studies. He was on his own now, but humbly depending on God. He began by timidly asking the questions in simple Fijian and having the Fijians read the answers from the Bible. It made him sweat, but it was fun. Not only was John Fulton learning to preach in Fijian in this way, but some of the Fijians were learning to read, and reading from the Word of God brought conviction to their hearts.

Step by step they had opened their hearts to receive the dear Lord Jesus. He had filled their hearts with love—love for one another and love for Him—and they gladly showed their love by obedience to God's commandments, and by cleansing their body temples by giving up the use of tobacco, *yang-gona,* and unclean meats. They met for Sabbath school and church each Sabbath day at the Fultons' home.

As the interest grew, John realized more and more that he must have a boat of some kind to visit the eighty inhabited islands in the Fiji group, and also to visit the many villages on the banks of the great rivers. So he wrote to friends in

New Zealand, Australia, and America, and finally succeeded in getting together eighty pounds for this project.

As for John Cole, the trip home did him good, and before long he was hard at work in Oregon. Almost at once he made stereopticon slides from photographic negatives of pictures he had taken in Pitcairn, Norfolk, and Fiji. He gave illustrated lectures in schoolhouses and churches anywhere and everywhere he could. He took up collections and began building up a fund to buy a small printing press to make one of his dreams for Fiji come true. He also wrote to the General Conference urging them to send another missionary couple to help the Fultons in Fiji, and by February of 1898 he had the pleasure of hearing that they had chosen C. H. Parker and his wife, Myrtle, to go to Fiji, and that they would be ready to leave about the middle of the year. He wrote the good news to John Fulton, but the letter he received in reply made his heart ache. "The work is progressing splendidly," it said, "and I am almost able to preach in Fijian, but poor Susie is not well. Those eleven months of privation were just too much for her. It seems impossible for her to get back her strength, and the doctor is urging me to take her home for a furlough. Edith will have to go home to New Zealand for a few months. I will take Susie, the two girls, and Baby George to Grandma Newlon's home in Bishop, California, then I will come right back, for I cannot bear to leave these dear people alone for long."

"Poor John," sighed John Cole as he read the letter to Fanny. "What a price some of us have to pay for the little we are able to do for the Lord!"

"But remember," Fanny replied, "a living dog is better than a dead lion. You'll see. Susie will be back in Fiji again before too long, and so might we! We are not dead yet!"

And so it came to pass that in March, 1898, John and

Susie Fulton with their two little girls, Jessie, six, Agnes, four and a half, and eleven-month-old Georgie got on the boat in Suva and sailed back home on their first furlough. Before leaving, however, John placed an order with a reliable boat-builder in Suva for a yacht thirty feet long and ten feet wide. He hoped that it would be ready for use by the time he returned.

The trip home was pleasant and did them good. An abundance of milk and fruit and homemade bread in Grandma Newlon's home soon had them all feeling fit again.

John Fulton wrote to the Parkers right away, and when he learned that they were booked to leave Portland, Oregon, for Fiji early in July, he said to Susie, "I'm going back with them. I've been away too long already. I can be of help to the Parkers. I can begin teaching them Fijian on the way."

"Can't we come too?" begged Susie.

"No! No!" said John. "You and the children stay a few more months. You all need it more than I do. But just think, Susie, since the boat is leaving from Portland I'll have another visit with John and Fanny Cole!" And he did. In June he went to Portland, Oregon. There he met the Parkers and visited with his old friends the Coles. They talked about old Ambrose, and the new believers. They talked about the press-to-be and rejoiced in the evidences they had that God was renewing their health and strength.

John Fulton was delighted with the Parkers. Calvin was a young man his own age, twenty-nine. They had a little girl two years old named Ramona, and Mrs. Parker had had some nurse's training in the Battle Creek Sanitarium.

John Fulton could hardly wait to get back to dear old Fiji. Right on schedule they boarded the S. S. *Warrimo* in Portland, and on the predetermined day landed in Suva early in August.

"Maybe it will be better for us to have two missions, Cal-

vin," suggested John as they talked over their plans. "But anyway you will live in the Coles's house till we decide where
your station shall be."

"That's all right with us," replied Calvin. "We will do
whatever you think is best."

"Fortunately," added John, "the little yacht that I ordered
before taking Mrs. Fulton home is all finished and is seaworthy. I have named it the *Thina,* which means 'lamp.' "

"Splendid!" said Calvin.

By this time Edith, who was now seventeen, was back from
New Zealand. She entered enthusiastically into the work of
outfitting the yacht, and soon had sleeping quarters for five,
and a foldaway kitchen with a Primus stove all ready for use.
John had no difficulty in hiring a crew of five Fijian men to
operate the yacht, from among those who were interested in
the truth.

One day not long after they had arrived, the missionaries
all got on board and set out on an itinerary among the islands.
They sailed in a northeasterly direction after leaving Suva
harbor and touched in at the tiny island of Mbau where the
old cannibal king Thakombau used to have his headquarters.
They saw the council house where the twenty-one Tongans
were buried alive in the post holes. They saw the stone in the
Wesleyan church on which Thakombau used to have his victims' heads smashed. They listened, horrified, as John Fulton
regaled them with stories of atrocities before the Fijians became Christians.

They sailed on to the island of Ovalau and stayed a few
days in the harbor of Levuka. This was the place where John
Cole had first started his work. Returning to Viti Levu, they
took a short trip up the Rewa River to become acquainted
with some of the inland towns and villages.

Calvin Parker was delighted to see the interest in the

open-air meetings that John Fulton was able to call together,
and rejoiced in John's ability to tell the simple story of Christ's
second coming in the Fijian language. They studied the possi-
bility of establishing the second mission station in several
places, but when they got back home they had come to no
conclusion.

Then one Sunday they sailed across the bay to Suva Vou.
"This is where Ratu Ambrose lives," said John. "Remember
how we have been warned to look out for the old chief, for
he will do anything for money. Well, he appears to be interested
in the truth. He attends every meeting we hold here."

"That's good," commented Calvin.

They walked up the hillside into the village. But before
they had come to the chief's house, they noticed that Ratu
Ambrose had come outside to greet them. *"Sa mbula! Sa
mbula* ["Are you well"]?" he cried. "I'm so glad you came
today, Misi Fulitoni. It is Sunday, and you shall preach in my
church."

John Fulton introduced the new missionaries. They had a
pleasant visit, then they all went into the church for a service.
It was actually John's first real sermon in Fijian in a church,
and he felt a little nervous. But God was with him and he
preached that day on the second coming of Christ with more
than human power.

"Come again," begged Ratu Ambrose when the meeting
was over. "Now you can preach in our language we want to
hear more about the Word of God, and about the *Lotu Savasava.*
Come and stay two or three weeks and teach us every day."

"Maybe your missionaries wouldn't like us to stay so long
and hold so many meetings," said John.

"It's *my* church. *I* built it," said Ratu Ambrose emphatically. "I have the right to ask you to come, and I want you to
come and stay a long time."

On the way back home John and Calvin talked things over. In spite of the warnings they had been given about the old chief, this seemed to be a definite leading of Providence. Why shouldn't they go and hold a three-week evangelistic effort there? Why not? The more they thought about it, the more certain they became that God was leading, so three weeks later the missionaries boarded the *Thina* again, and sailed across Suva Bay to Suva Vou. They slept and ate some of their meals on their little boat, but most of the time was spent with the Fijians in their homes. Mrs. Parker was adept at giving fomentations and with Edith as a translator, and a bag filled with bandages, disinfectants, eye drops, and ointments, she won the hearts of the women and children at once. While the sick ones flocked around Mrs. Parker, Edith told Bible stories to the children, and they loved it.

Each day the two men held a morning and an evening service and visited with the menfolk. It was an ideal way for Calvin to be learning to speak and read Fijian.

For three weeks the meetings continued. Ratu Ambrose attended the meetings faithfully. Yet in spite of John's hopes and faith, every time he saw him, into his mind there flashed the warning words, "Look out for old Ratu Ambrose."

Finally they came to the consecration service on the last Sabbath morning of their effort, and Ratu Ambrose was there. After an earnest appeal for those who were willing to obey God at all costs to "come out and be separate," in order to get ready to meet the Lord Jesus Christ at His second coming, John called for a season of prayer. One who prayed was Metui, an old fisherman, whose body still bore the scars of the terrible lacerations made when Ratu Ambrose had made him lie on the beach when he launched his canoe, and used his body as a roller. He prayed that God would take all the hard feelings from his heart. Then he prayed for his chief, Ambrose, that God would

Ratu Ambrose and his wife.

give him a new heart and make him a great light among his people.

After Metui had prayed, to everyone's surprise Ratu Ambrose prayed! "Look out!" the warning words began to flash into John Fulton's mind, but they were instantly eradicated by the old man's earnest prayer. He prayed that God would forgive him for his past wicked life and his harsh treatment of the village folk. Then his voice choked up. The tears rolled down his cheeks. He sobbed like a child—"And, O God, forgive me for being so cruel to my dear wife. I've been such a wicked man. But, God, I want a new heart. I want to be kind and good. O God, help me to be ready when Jesus comes."

When the season of prayer was over, the old chief stood up, and with the tears still running down his face, confessed his sins. He assured the people that he was finished with his old dishonest ways, that he was through with whisky, *yanggona,* and unclean foods, and that from now on he was going to be a real Christian. Suddenly, as he spoke John knew that this was not the old Ratu Ambrose anymore, but it was a new Ratu Ambrose —a new man in Christ Jesus.

The next morning before they left, Ratu Ambrose and a group of the village elders approached our two missionaries and said, "Look, Misi Fulitoni, you are looking for a place to build a mission station for Misi Parker. Why not build here in Suva Vou? We want you to live here always."

"Well," said Pastor Parker, "we were thinking of someplace farther away from Suva."

"But we want you here!" declared Ratu Ambrose.

"Yes, but——"

"Then do you know what I am going to do?" interrupted the chief seriously. "I'm going to hope that a great cyclone blows your houses to pieces, carries the pieces over and casts them down in Suva Vou, and puts them together right here in our midst."

"Well, of course," said Pastor Parker with a big smile on his face, "if that happened, we would just have to build our mission station here."

And as they sailed back home across the bay to Suva, John Fulton and Calvin Parker wondered if after all God was not behind the old chief's suggestion. Regularly each week they made the trip to worship with the new believers and to get them ready for baptism. On each occasion Ratu Ambrose was there to greet them.

"Well, how is the battle against liquor and unclean foods going?" inquired John seriously.

"God has taken away my desire for them all," the chief reported.

"Then what's that tobacco pipe doing in your pocket?"

"Oh, must that go too?" he asked as if it had never occurred to him before.

"Can you imagine the Lord Jesus smoking a pipe?" asked John.

"No! No! and I can't imagine *you* smoking a pipe, either. But some of our old missionaries smoked, and all the government men smoke."

"But Ratu, ours is the *Lotu Savasava,* and none of our members smoke."

"All right then," replied Ratu Ambrose, "away it goes." And he took his pipe and his tobacco out of his pocket and threw them away as far as he could, and he never touched them again.

A few weeks later at one of the meetings, Ratu Ambrose's wife, Andi Kilara, stood up and said, "I want to say something. I haven't been interested in the *Lotu Savasava* and I haven't come to many of the meetings, but it is different now, and I want to get ready for baptism too. It's all because of him!" and she cast a loving look at Ratu Ambrose. "He used to be such a monster. He used to get drunk and beat me. He was untrue to me. He made me do all the work in the garden. But it has all changed since he decided to join the *Lotu Savasava*. He never drinks now. He never gets angry with me or beats me anymore. He works in the garden with me and he is kind and true to me. He brings home all his money. He loves his Bible, and when I hear him praying for me, it makes me cry for joy. So I told him the other day, 'Your God will be my God too. Your *lotu* will be my *lotu*. We will be baptized together and go to the *Lotu Savasava* together, and go to heaven together.' " There is no need to say that this heartfelt testimony brought great joy to everyone.

"Do you know, John," said Calvin one day as they were returning from one of those meetings, "I am impressed more and more that perhaps we should locate our mission station at Suva Vou."

"I feel the same way, Calvin," replied John.

"Then let us decide to do so at once."

"All right, Calvin. You can move into my house, and we will carefully take your house apart and rebuild it at Suva Vou."

When they told Ratu Ambrose of their decision, he wept for joy. "God has sent the cyclone at last," he exclaimed. "And now you will live in our midst." Through the chief's influence many willing workers came to help, and in a little more than a month the Parkers were living in the rebuilt mission home in Suva Vou.

In November of that year the believers there, including Ratu Ambrose and Andi Kilara, together with the believers from Tamavua, were baptized in the Lami River that flows by Suva Vou. This was the first baptism in Fiji, and the following Sabbath, Pastor Fulton held the first communion service with the newly organized church.

The new members had never before seen or taken part in the ordinance of foot washing. In simple language Pastor

Fulton explained how sin and sorrow were all the result of the pride which Lucifer had in his heart. He told of the plan the Lord Jesus Himself had put in the early Christian church, to keep pride out of the hearts of His followers. Then he told how Jesus Himself had washed the feet of His disciples, and had said, "If I then, your Lord and Master, have washed your feet; ye also ought to wash one another's feet. . . . If ye know these things, happy are ye if ye do them."

The women then retired to a nearby house for their service. Left alone with the men, John girded himself with a towel and picked up a basin of water to show the new believers how the foot washing was done. As he did so he kept watching Ratu Ambrose. He wondered what this great chief would do. All his life he had been accustomed to being served by others. What would he do now? There was no need to worry about it, however, for suddenly the old chief got the idea. He sprang to his feet, and girding himself with a towel, said, "Misi Fulitoni, please let me wash their feet." Taking a basin of water, he knelt first at the feet of Metui, the poor old fisherman whose body still bore the marks of his cruelty, and prepared to wash his feet.

"No! No!" cried Metui in anguish. "You must not wash my feet! You are a great high chief and I am only a common man!" It was a tense moment. The men sitting there trembled with emotion, partly from fear, partly from joy. Some began to weep. But Ratu Ambrose was speaking again. They held their breath to hear what he would say. "Metui," he said softly, "you must let me wash your feet, for there is no chief here today, only Jesus."

O what joy! Jesus was indeed there that day by the presence of His Holy Spirit and the young missionaries felt that the foundations of the *Lotu Savasava* were being divinely established.

A few weeks later John stepped into Mr. Bailey's shoe shop in Suva. Mr. Bailey was an infidel and had no time for, or interest in, religion, but this day he said to Mr. Fulton, "Whatever has come over old Ambrose?"

"Why do you ask?" inquired John. "What has he done?"

"I don't know what has happened to him. I only know that he has owed me two pounds ten shillings [$12.50 at that time] for years and I never expected to see a penny of it. But the other day he came in and put the whole sum of money down in front of me and said, 'Misi Bailey, here is the money I have owed you so long.'"

"Well, you know," said John with a smile, "converted men pay their debts."

Mr. Bailey felt uneasy for a moment, then said, "Converted or not, I don't know anything about that, but I was sure glad to get my two pounds ten." But after John left the thought persisted in Mr. Bailey's mind, There must be something to this *Lotu Savasava* if it can do that to old Ratu Ambrose.

Of course, the dear old man still had much to learn. One day he brought John ten shillings ($2.50 at that time) for tithe. He had paid his regular tithe only a few days before, so John said to him, "Well, Ratu, God is blessing you for paying your tithe, isn't He?"

"Yes," he replied, "the Lord surely did bless me. I was over in Suva and I played a game of billiards with two Englishmen, and I won five pounds!"

"Do you mean to say you were over there in a saloon playing billiards?" asked John, trying to suppress his chagrin.

"But, Misi Fulitoni, I didn't drink or smoke. Is it wrong to gamble? You never told me it was wrong to gamble."

"I didn't think I needed to tell you that the *Lotu Savasava* keeps away from all the snares of Satan."

"All right!" said Ambrose as simply as a child would say it. "Then away goes gambling along with pork and whisky and tobacco." And he never gambled again.

No wonder Mr. Scott, a government official, said to Mr. Fulton one day, "The government is keeping its eye on old Ratu Ambrose. He has been such a rascal and such a rogue. You know, he was once a government officer. He was very popular. He even went to Australia on government business and got his name and his picture in the papers. But the temptation was too great. He took to drinking. He embezzled government funds, lost his position, and was imprisoned. But now look at him! He is so different! He is like a new man!"

"Yes," agreed John Fulton, "Mr. Scott, he *is* a new man."

Pauliasi Bunoa, the first Seventh-
day Adventist ordained minister in
the South Sea Islands. He was ordained in 1906.

Pauliasi Bunoa

AMONG THOSE WHO attended the series of meetings in Suva Vou in September, 1898, there was also a Fijian Wesleyan minister by the name of Pauliasi Bunoa. He could remember the first Wesleyan missionaries visiting and holding meetings in his father's home on the island of Lakemba, when he was just seven years old. His father and his father's friends were, of course, all cannibals, but the gospel of the love of God won its way into the hearts of a number of them and they openly declared themselves to be Christians.

Immediately the other islanders turned on them and threatened to kill them. So Bunoa's father and his Christian friends had to flee for their lives to some mountain caves. They hid there for a year till the anger of the others cooled down and they dared to return to their families again. Bunoa himself waited till he was full grown, then he declared himself to be a Christian. When he was baptized he added the new name Pauliasi (Paul) to his old name Bunoa. He went to a Christian school, married a Christian young woman, and became a Christian worker. A few years later he was ordained and sent as a missionary to the cannibals of New Ireland and New Britain off the coast of New Guinea. There he remained for ten years, but fever and sickness claimed his children one by one, and last of all his faithful wife, so that he was left all alone, and finally returned to Fiji.

At Suva Vou he met a Christian widow who had one daughter. They were married and he was put in charge of a district. His headquarters were in Suva, and the Wesleyan church in Suva Vou was in his district, so naturally he was at the meetings that John Fulton and Calvin Parker held there. At this time he was in his late fifties, and had three lovely girls in his family. He was amazed at the way Bible prophecy was being fulfilled in world events. He was astonished at the new light that shone from the Word of God. And he was perplexed as to why *his* missionaries hadn't taught these things. He became convinced that the teaching of the *Lotu Savasava* was right, but he was not ready to take his stand when Ratu Ambrose did.

He needed more time to study and to make sure. So one evening after the meeting he visited with John Fulton and said, "Misi Fulitoni, have you any tracts in Fijian or books in Fijian so that I could study more?"

"Oh, Pauliasi," replied John, "I'm sorry but we have no tracts or books yet. However, I am right now doing my best to prepare an eight-page tract on the true Bible Sabbath. But my Fijian is so faulty. I need a Fijian scholar to correct my Fijian words."

"Then, Misi Fulitoni," said Pauliasi, "would you let me correct your writing? I don't know much English, but I am a graduate from the Fijian Seminary and I would be glad to put your words into good Fijian."

"Why, Pauliasi!" exclaimed John Fulton in surprise. "I have been praying for someone to come along who would do just that. And now God has answered my prayers."

So Pauliasi Bunoa came to John Fulton's home and painstakingly smoothed out John's somewhat awkward sentences. As he did so his eyes brightened. He asked many pertinent questions, then wrote quickly in correct Fijian. Pauliasi was an expert scholar indeed and soon John's eight-page tract was completed in fluent Fijian. But still Pauliasi continued to ask questions, so John decided to write some more and make it a sixteen-page tract. Day after day they studied. Day after day Pauliasi asked questions and wrote down the thoughts in fluent Fijian. At last there was material enough for the sixteen-page tract, but it was evident that Pauliasi was becoming more and more troubled about the Sabbath question, and he still asked questions. So John decided to make it a thirty-two page tract, and by the time it was finished they had an excellent treatise on the Sabbath and Satan's attempt to change it from the seventh day to Sunday. They named it *Singa ni Vakathengu* ("Day of Rest"), and mailed the precious manuscript to the Pacific Press in Oakland, California, where it was printed and returned to Fiji posthaste.

By this time Pauliasi was "almost persuaded," and found himself in an awkward situation. Here he was, still a Wesleyan minister, keeping company with Seventh-day Adventists. He couldn't belong to both churches! What could he do? He went to John Fulton and asked, "Do you need me anymore, Misi Fulitoni, now that the tract is finished?"

"Indeed I do, Pauliasi," replied John. "Now I want to start translating a small book of Bible studies. And when that is done I want to translate a large book called *The Great Controversy.*"

A book! The idea struck home at once. This was just what he wanted. So it took only a second for Pauliasi to make up his mind and say, "I will be very glad to keep on assisting you." Thus it was that a happy and profitable friendship was formed between the two men and their families.

Here we must pause a moment to introduce another young man by the name of Alipati ("Albert") Rainima. He had been won by the preaching of John Cole and was actually the first Fijian to begin to keep the Sabbath. He was a promising young fellow, and one day delighted John Fulton by saying, "Misi Fulitoni, a man tried to argue with me the other day that sprinkling was enough and that we need not be immersed for baptism. He said when Jesus said, 'Suffer the children to come unto me,' He was actually baptizing them by sprinkling. How would you answer that?"

John thought quickly and said, "Well, Alipati, the Bible simply says that Jesus placed His hands on their heads and blessed them."

"Yes, but isn't there a text to prove that Jesus was not baptizing them?"

"I don't think of a text just now," said John.

"Well, I know one. And it shut that man up quickly and he couldn't say anything more."

"Which text?"

"John 4:2. It says plainly, 'Jesus himself baptized not, but his disciples.'"

"That satisfies me too!" said John with a smile, then added, "Alipati, keep on studying the good old Book and you'll be a preacher someday."

"That's what I want to be, Misi Fulitoni," said Alipati earnestly. And from that moment Alipati became one of John's close friends also.

Toward the end of 1898 John received a most encouraging letter from John Cole. "At last I have it!" the letter said. "A beautiful little Columbian hand lever press! It will print a page 8 inches by 12 inches or two pages 8 inches by six inches. I'm sending a font of type and a type case also. To keep it from rattling around in its packing case I am stuffing the empty spaces with prunes! It will be part of the freight on the *Pitcairn* which is leaving here on its sixth journey to the South Seas, January 22."

You can imagine the joy this letter brought to the missionaries in Fiji. "John, I think you ought to move your house over here to Suva Vou," urged Calvin Parker excitedly. "When we get into the printing business we will need to be close together. You will be the editor, Pauliasi will be the translator, and you'll need a printer's devil. I will make a good printer's devil, don't you think? And Edith can help set the type."

"Say, Calvin, I think you've got it. It sounds like a good idea to me," said John happily. "And I have more good news. My wife and children are coming back on the February boat, and Susie is bringing her mother who plans to stay with us for a year. That just about gives me time to take my house apart and rebuild it in Suva Vou before they get here."

It was a good idea. Myrtle Parker, Edith, and even little Ramona joined in the rejoicing at the thought of having missionary companions living together on the main mission station.

John and a company of Fijian workmen immediately got to work, and little by little the Fulton house was dismantled and rebuilt in Suva Vou. By February all was ready.

In due time the boat from America arrived, and sure enough, Susie, her children, and her mother were on board looking the picture of health. The Parkers, Edith, John, Pauliasi, and Alipati were on the wharf to meet them. What a welcome they were given! Shouts of joy from the children, loving embraces and tears of joy from everybody.

"You will be escorted to your new home in our own mission yacht, the *Thina*," said John proudly. And as soon as the customs officers cleared their luggage it was loaded onto the mission boat and they sailed joyfully across the bay to their new home at Suva Vou.

For a month or two all was joy and gladness. The men were getting a place ready for the printing press that was on its way. Pauliasi and Alipati were enthusiastically helping to place their new Fijian tract *Singa ni Vakathengu* in the hands of their friends and all who were interested. Ratu Ambrose was as pleased about the new developments as he could be. Then, one day something happened that brought as much anguish to them all as if a bomb had been dropped in their midst. It was a letter from Elder Daniells, the president of the Australian Union Conference. "Dear Brother Fulton," it said, "As the work is progressing in Australia we find it advantageous to organize a new conference for the State of Queensland, and we are unanimous in inviting you to be the president of this new conference."

"No! No!" said John to himself as his heart pounded and his face flushed.

"No! No!" said Susie when he read the letter to her.

"No! No!" said the Parkers.

"No! No!" said Pauliasi and Alipati. And Ratu Ambrose added as tears rolled down his face, "We cannot let you go. You belong to us. We need you more than they do!"

John wrote to the General Conference appealing to them to grant him the privilege of remaining in Fiji as a humble missionary rather than being transferred to Queensland as a conference president.

"John, do you know what I think?" Susie remarked one day as they waited for the reply from the General Conference.

"What do you think, my dear?" asked John affectionately.

"Well, you know about the three temptations—appetite, faith, and ambition."

"Yes."

"Well, we've had the temptation on appetite. Maybe this is the temptation on ambition."

"Maybe it is."

"Just think, you could be a *big* president of a conference and live in a nice house and have plenty of——"

"Susie! Susie! Get thee behind me!" said John playfully. "What joy could be greater than this? We'll soon have our press. You and Edith have already translated some hymns. We'll soon be able to print them. Calvin can't preach in Fijian yet, Pauliasi hasn't quite taken his stand yet, and dear old Ratu Ambrose—oh, how can I leave them? I am sure the General Conference will let us stay."

And Susie added, "And I am sure you have overcome your temptation on ambition."

In due time the letter from the General Conference came, granting them the privilege of staying on in Fiji, and about the same time the *Pitcairn* arrived with their precious little printing press all packed securely in prunes!

With great jubilation the Columbian lever press was set up in a corner of the Parkers' house, and they all started on their new duties as press workers. John had had a little experience setting type at Healdsburg College. The others had had no experience at all, but that didn't stop them. Calvin rolled up his sleeves, put on an apron, and started right in being a printer's devil. He was a *bad* devil to begin with. He set the type from left to right as when typewriting, so that it came out backwards when printed. He sometimes let his type stick slip and made "pie"—lead pie—which took much time to straighten out. But he learned by experience and it was not too long before he was a *good* devil.

Edith did better, and soon the rhythmic throb of the press as the boys fed in the sheets of paper and pulled down the lever, sounded like music in their ears. Their first creation was a small hymnbook, and how the members of the *Lotu Savasava* enjoyed singing the good old Adventist hymns! Then there

followed a small book of Bible studies on Daniel two and the
signs of Christ's second coming.

"Well, Pauliasi," said John one day, "how do you like our
press now?"

"It is very good, Misi Fulitoni," he replied. "But I am very
heavy-hearted."

"Why is that, Pauliasi?"

"Well, I find in my heart two great desires. I want to do
what the Bible tells me to do, and I want the Bible to tell me
that what I have been doing is right. I have visited the English
missionaries of my church. They say that Christ changed the
Sabbath but they cannot give me one text from the Bible that
says so. They say that the seventh-day Sabbath was only for
the Jews, but they cannot give me one text that says so. They
say that the *Lotu Savasava* is only a little *lotu* and it will soon
disappear. But it is not disappearing, it is growing larger and
larger."

"And the *Lotu Savasava* has a Bible text for everything it
preaches and for everything it does," added John.

"I know," replied Pauliasi, "so my heart is heavy. I don't
know what to do."

"Let me give you another text," said John earnestly. For he
felt the time had come for Pauliasi to make a definite decision.
"Maybe this text will take away your burden. It is James 4:17.
'Therefore to him that knoweth to do good, and doeth it not,
to him it is sin.'"

"Then am I a sinner?" he asked a little angrily. And without waiting to hear more, he abruptly turned and went away.
For a moment John wondered if he had spoken wisely, but before long Pauliasi was back again. His face was all smiles. "It's
true! It's true!" he said. "It was the Word of God that said I
was a sinner. But I have surrendered myself to God and His
Word, and my burden has been taken away. Now I know what

I am going to do." Not long after this Pauliasi was baptized, and then everyone knew that he was truly a Seventh-day Adventist.

His Wesleyan friends were disappointed that such an able scholar had joined the *Lotu Savasava,* and the Wesleyan European missionaries did all they could to persuade him to come back and to prevent others from following him.

One Sunday the European mission superintendent from Suva came to preach in the Suva Vou Wesleyan church in defense of the Sunday cause. Pastor Fulton happened to be away, but Pauliasi, and Ratu Ambrose, and Alipati, and a number of our church members were there. They listened attentively to the usual arguments that are given for resting on Sunday.

At the close of the sermon the preacher walked down the aisle to where Pauliasi was sitting. "I am very sorry, Pauliasi," he said, "that you have turned away from the church you have served and upheld so long as a preacher and as a missionary."

"I am sorry too," replied Pauliasi, "but the Bible has driven me to this decision."

"But didn't you understand my sermon this morning?" asked the missionary.

"Oh, yes, I understood. But you gave only words of man to support your arguments. You gave no texts from the Bible." They were speaking in Fijian so the whole congregation could hear and understand what they were saying. "Brother Missionary," went on Pauliasi, "if you could give me just one 'Thus saith the Lord' commanding us to keep Sunday I would come back to my old church at once."

The European missionary stood helpless for a moment, for of course there is no such "Thus saith the Lord." Then Pauliasi under the inspiration of the Holy Spirit said very humbly, "Brother Missionary, you are not the judge over this Sabbath law, and neither am I the judge. But if in the great day of judg-

8

ment I am found to be wrong, I am going to bring a charge against Jehovah because He wrote with His own finger the law of the Ten Commandments, the fourth of which says the seventh day is the Sabbath, and we are commanded to keep it. And if found to be wrong I will bring a charge against all the patriarchs and prophets of Old Testament times because they all taught the seventh-day Sabbath and kept it. And I will also bring a charge against the Lord Jesus Christ, who on the mount said, 'Think not that I am come to destroy the law . . . : I am not come to destroy, but to fulfill.' And Jesus kept His Father's commandments and rested on the holy Sabbath, and preached in the synagogues. And if I am found to be wrong, I'll also bring a charge against the apostle Paul, who said of the law that it was holy, just, and good, and he also honored the Sabbath day by preaching in the synagogue on that day, as well as by the riverside. In short, if I am wrong, I'll bring charges against Jehovah, the patriarchs and prophets in Old Testament times, and against Jesus, Paul, and the apostles in New Testament times. And now, Brother Missionary, if *you* are found to be wrong over this Sunday question, what Bible characters are you going to bring charges against?"

There was absolute silence, and the preacher walked away discomfited. Pauliasi's argument was unanswerable. That day in the Fijian village of Suva Vou there were great searchings of heart. Young men had their interest quickened, and later some of them became preachers of the Word for the *Lotu Savasava*.

About this time John brought home another letter that produced quite a little excitement. "Susie! Susie!" he called as he rushed into the house. "Guess what! A letter from Robert and Henrietta!"

Susie dropped what she was doing. The children, attracted by their father's enthusiasm, came rushing in and gathered around. "Quick, let me have it!" said Susie.

"All right, here's your part," said John as he handed her a letter and a photograph.

"Oh, John, it's a picture of Henrietta's family," exclaimed Susie before taking time to read the letter. "Oh look! There's dear old Henrietta! The same sweet motherly girl! And there's Robert. He hasn't changed much. But look at the children! The big boy is Reuben. He is a few years older than Jessie."

"Let me see! Let me see!" shouted seven-year-old Jessie.

"And the second boy is Eric. He's about the same age as Agnes."

"Let me see! Let me see!" shouted five-year-old Agnes.

"And this is Baby Ruth. Just a year older than our two-year-old Georgie."

"Let me see! Let me see!" cried nineteen-year-old Edith. "Oh aren't they sweet!"

"It is interesting, John, isn't it?" said Susie somewhat thoughtfully. "The Hares have two boys and a girl and we have two girls and a boy! Wouldn't it be wonderful if——"

"If what?" asked John.

"Oh, nothing! I was just dreaming," said Susie, and she changed the subject. "Now what does your letter from Robert say?"

"Well, you know Robert was made editor of the Australian paper *The Bible Echo* last year."

"Yes," said Susie, "I've noticed his articles and his poems. He is doing a good job."

"He is indeed. But he is demanding that I write some articles for his *Bible Echo,* and where could I find time to——"

"But, John, you must. Just for old friendship's sake."

"I suppose I should," agreed John. And he did. "And Susie, you ought to send Henrietta a picture of *our* family, just for old friendship's sake."

"I suppose I should!" agreed Susie fondly. And she did.

"You know, Susie, we'll be having our own Fijian paper one of these days," said John as they talked things over. "And we will translate some of Robert's articles and put them in our paper!"

"A good idea!" agreed Susie. "When are you going to start our paper?"

"Ever since our press got to working, the conviction has deepened in my heart that we should publish our own paper as soon as possible. And now we have the press, and we know how to work it. Pauliasi can smooth out the rough translations that I make. I don't see why we couldn't start the first of next year."

"Have you decided on a name for it yet?"

"Yes, *Rarama* ["light"]. How do you like that?"

"Why, that is splendid."

"And Pauliasi says that with a boat called *Thina* ["lamp"] and a monthly paper called *Rarama* we can really wake up old Fiji. And Alipati can hardly wait. He says he will put his full time in selling *Rarama*."

So it was that in January, 1900, the first copy of the *Rarama* came off the little old Columbia lever press. What a day of rejoicing it was.

It wasn't quite as easy, however, as it sounds. Their only composing stone was a piece of broken plate glass from one of the stores in Suva. There was no material for making the rollers available in Suva, so John resorted to making the rollers from glue, molasses, and glycerine according to a recipe he found in a book on printing. Borrowing a big saucepan from Susie, he set to work and soon had the mixture stewing on the kitchen stove. Unfortunately, it had a very putrid odor, and when some of the abominable conglomeration boiled over and filled the house with smoke and smudge, Susie couldn't stand it one more minute.

"John Fulton," she said vehemently, "take this stuff out! You're not going to fill my nice house with your unholy mess!"

John made no reply. He knew when he was not wanted, and he retreated with all speed to an obscure corner in a nearby shed. There with the help of a little Primus stove he finished cooking the horrible stuff. But believe it or not, when at last he poured the material into the well-greased molds, to his great delight it made excellent rollers, and they worked! And the *Rarama* came off the press as pretty as you could wish for. They had no paper cutter to trim the edges, but that didn't matter. An old straight-edge razor served the purpose.

Thus the *Rarama* was born, and a new day had dawned for old Fiji.

Amazed at the Mighty Power of God

ONE OF THE REWARDS promised in Revelation 2:17 to God's overcoming saints is the giving of a new name when they are taken to heaven. But in Fiji they are not content to wait till they go to heaven to receive a new name. They want a new name as soon as they are baptized and become Christians. Of course, the favorite place to find these new names is the Bible, though some of them, especially the women, may decide on the name of a favorite missionary. So it was that Pastor Fulton found himself confronted with many a request for a new name as he studied with his candidates for baptism.

Frequently they found their own names and only asked for his opinion. The names Pita ("Peter"), Jemesa ("James"), Joni ("John"), Patolomeo ("Bartholomew"), and the other disciples were very commonly used. They also selected names from among the Old Testament characters. The names of Keni ("Cain"), Epeli ("Abel"), and Sethi ("Seth") were often chosen. The names of the kings and the prophets, such as Saula ("Saul"), Tevita ("David"), Solomoni ("Solomon"), Taniela ("Daniel") and Maika ("Micah"), were great favorites. But sometimes John was amazed at some of the choices that were made by some of the new converts. Imagine how he felt when one of the young men said, "I have chosen the name Asaseli ["Azazel"]."

"But that means scapegoat!" John pointed out with real concern.

"I know. But no one else has that name, Misi Fulitoni, and I like it."

Another young man said, "Misi Fulitoni, I also have chosen a name I've never heard before."

"What is it?" asked John.

"Pelisipupi ["Beelzebub"]," he replied.

"But Pelisipupi means 'prince of devils'!" said John.

"But they called Jesus that name," he pleaded, "and I don't have to be a bad Pelisipupi." And so Asaseli and Pelisipupi they were named!

There was another old saint who lived on the north side of Viti Levu, who also wanted a new name—a name no one else had ever chosen.

"What about Eparama ["Abraham"], Isaki ["Isaac"], or Jekope ["Jacob"]?" suggested John.

"No, no! There are plenty of them everywhere," replied the old man sadly.

"Well what about Mathiu ["Matthew"], Marika ["Mark"], Luki ["Luke"], or Joni ["John"]?"

"No, no! I've heard all those."

Then John got a brain storm. "Well, what about Luke's friend—his special friend for whom he wrote the book of Luke?"

"Who was he? I've never heard of him."

"Theofilo ["Theophilus"]. Luke called him most excellent Theofilo!"

The old man's eyes brightened, a smile lighted up his face. "*Vinaka! Vinaka! Vinaka sara* ["Good, good, very good"]!"

he cried. "I've never heard of anyone called Theofilo before.
That will be my new name."

Another old man looked and looked and thought and
thought for a long time, then finally settled on Terah, the name
of Abraham's father. Old Terah had actually been a cannibal.
He had eaten human flesh. "Did you think *mbokola* tasted
good in those days?" asked John.

"Those were days of darkness," he replied. "Now the very
thought of it fills me with disgust."

Some time later old Terah was buying a copy of our
Fijian *Great Controversy*. His friends laughed at him. "What
are *you* buying a book for?" they said in derision. "You can't
read!"

"I know I cannot read," he replied humbly, "but I can look
at the pictures, can't I? And some of my children will read it
to me." So Terah bought the book and his children did read it
to him. I'm sure the father of Abraham would have been proud
if he could have been there when the church was organized in
his village and Terah was selected one of the deacons.

Let me tell you of an amazing thing that God did for one of
these old saints, and also of an amazing thing that this old saint
did for God. He had taken the name of Tevita when he became
a Christian, and his wife's name was Anareta. It is difficult to
say just how old Tevita was when John first met him. The Fijians in those days kept no records of births, but an estimate
could be made by asking how big they were when the Fiji Islands were ceded to Britain (1874), or when the measles epidemic swept away 40,000 Fijians in the early days after the
British first settled there (about 1860).

Since Tevita was a young man at the time of the measles
epidemic, he must have been in his late fifties, and he had a
family of six fine young people—Taniela ("Daniel"), Timothi
("Timothy"), Setereki ("Shadrach"), Jemesa ("James"), Maika

Seventh-day Adventist church at Suva Vou.

A portion of the village of Suva Vou, Fiji, near the headquarters of the Fiji Mission.

("Micah"), and a daughter Liviana. Tevita was an old man and had lost practically all of his teeth, but that was not all. Some years before a piece of heavy lumber had fallen on him and had permanently injured his spine so that he was a pathetic looking cripple who had to hobble about with two canes. Yet in spite of his physical infirmity, Tevita was a good man and loved God with all his heart.

Tevita's wife, Anareta, was a real character. She was a *vuniwai*, literally, "source of water." This is a name given to all village medicine doctors. Though Anareta was a nominal Christian she still clung to the old superstitions of the *vuniwais*. She believed that sickness and disease were caused by evil spirits entering the body to torment it. Therefore a cure demanded that some kind of torture be administered to drive the evil spirits out. The flesh was cut, or pierced with needles. The abdomen was often burned with coals of fire or red-hot stones, and the poor patients were forced to drink bitter and disgusting mixtures and concoctions. Anareta was an expert in all the ways of the *vuniwais*. She held a strange spell over the village folk, and was much sought after by Christians and heathen alike.

She tried all of her skill and incantations on poor old Tevita, but nothing did him any good, and with no teeth to chew his food he got thinner and thinner and weaker and weaker till he expected to die at any time.

It was about this time that Pastors Fulton and Parker held that series of meetings in Suva Vou we have previously referred to. Tevita and Anareta and their six grown children attended. They attended every meeting and they all took their stand for the truth at the same time that old Ratu Ambrose took his stand, and they were all baptized. They gave up their tobacco and *yanggona,* as well as pork and unclean fish. When the church was organized old Tevita was chosen as the elder, and as he took up his duties for God he began to improve in health.

"Anareta," he confided one day, "I'm getting better! My joints are not so stiff. I can walk better."

"Indeed and you are better," admitted Anareta. "The *Lotu Savasava* is making a new man out of you."

"That's it! That's it!" agreed old Tevita. "The third angel's message has given me new health!"

In a few months he was able to throw away one of his canes. "Now see what the third angel's message has done for me!" he cried exultantly. "Truly God has given me new truth and new health. How I thank Him for the third angel's message and for health reform!"

But God wasn't finished with old Tevita yet. Just when everything was going well and the little lever press was producing its early copies of the *Rarama*, Tevita's mouth began to feel sore. It hurt to even roll the mashed yams and taro around in his mouth before swallowing them.

"If we were not Seventh-day Adventists, I'd say it was the evil spirits!" declared Anareta.

"No! No! Not evil spirits!" Tevita declared stoutly.

"Better let me look," suggested Anareta. "Maybe it is gumboils in your mouth."

"Well, you can look. But, Anareta, I want none of your *vuniwai* humbug now, remember."

So Anareta looked. She put her fingers on the sore place and felt carefully. She rubbed gently and felt again. Then suddenly her eyes bugged out. She caught her breath, and gasped, "Tevita, old man, I do declare you are cutting a new tooth!"

Tevita was electrified. He sat up. "It can't be!" he cried. "I'm too old."

"Too old or not too old," declared Anareta, "you can't fool an old *vuniwai* like me. I have been feeling for babies' teeth all of my life, and as sure as I am alive I tell you, old man, you *are* cutting a tooth."

Tevita put his finger in his mouth and felt. Sure enough, there was a new tooth coming through. In a month or so, another came through, and then another, and they didn't stop coming through till he had a complete third set of pearly white teeth!

Tevita soon forgot about the feeling of soreness he had had in his mouth. He showed his new teeth to everyone who would look, and to everyone who would listen he would say, "First, God gave me the third angel's message. Then the third angel's message gave me my third set of teeth. Did you ever see or hear tell of anything like this in all your life?" When old Tevita preached you never heard a more inspiring sermon, and when he prayed you never heard a more fervent prayer. There was no question about it, Tevita knew God and walked with Him.

This is the amazing thing that God did for Tevita. Now listen while I tell you of an amazing thing that Tevita did for God.

One weekend John Fulton and Calvin Parker were away worshiping with another company of believers, and Tevita as church elder was asked to look after the services and preach the sermon for the Suva Vou church. There was to be a *meke* (a ceremonial dance) that Sabbath on the nearby village common or playground. The playground was a large cleared place in the center of the village, around which the houses were all built. Since the houses were so close to the playground, and since there was always so much drinking, noise, shouting, laughter, and play connected with these *mekes,* old Tevita wondered what he could do to keep his church members, especially his young people, out of the way of temptation. He talked earnestly with God about the problem, and God must have told him what to do, for that morning after the service he announced, "You all know there will be a *meke* on the village playground this afternoon at three o'clock. So in order to be out of temptation's way, the church *lali* will sound at three o'clock and we will have an afternoon service here in the church."

"*Vinaka! Vinaka* ["good, good"]!" responded the old ones.

"And you fathers and mothers make sure that not one of your children is missing at our service."

"*Vinaka! Vinaka!*" responded the fathers and the mothers. And at three o'clock, as the noise from the *meke* on the village playground began to sound, the church *lali* also sounded, Boom! boom! boom! boom! And the believers and their children came to church. Every one of them came. There was not one missing. They had a good song service. Then old Tevita preached till four o'clock. As he closed his sermon he listened for a moment. The sounds from the *meke* could still be heard, so old Tevita said, "The *meke* has not yet finished, and we ought not go near there on God's holy day. My sermon is over and I haven't a new one prepared, so I will preach this one over again."

He preached till five o'clock. Then he listened a moment. The sounds from the *meke* could still be heard. He said, "The *meke* is not yet finished, but I have preached my sermon twice, so I will not preach it again. But now I will let some of you say a word." And several of them did. They told of their joy in serving the Lord. They told of their hope of being ready when Jesus comes. Then they had a season of prayer. As they rose from their knees the sun was setting. They listened, but no sounds came from the playground. The *meke* was over, and with it the hours of temptation were past.

Amazing as it sounds, not one person left the church during that three-hour service. There was no doubt about it. God loved old Tevita, and he loved God.

Now let me tell you of another amazing evidence of the mighty power of God that was in that first Fijian tract, *Singa ni Vakathengu*, and the new-born periodical the *Rarama*.

On a little island just off the east coast of Viti Levu there lived a Christian trader by the name of Epenisa Reece. He had a wife and a married son. Epenisa owned a fair-sized sailing ship with which he traded cloth, sugar, soap, oil, and flour for copra (dried coconut meat) in the villages up and down the east coast of the large island, known as the Ra Coast. When his ship was fully loaded he would take the copra to Suva, sell it to the traders there, then load up again with cloth and other supplies for the return journey.

Well, one day while his ship was in Suva, our enthusiastic literature worker, Alipati, gave one of his sailors a copy of our first tract, *Singa ni Vakathengu*. The sailor looked it over and showed it to his companions, but since no one wanted to be bothered reading it, he crumpled it up and threw it down on the deck. Soon after this, Captain Epenisa came along. Seeing the crumpled up piece of paper, he picked it up, straightened it out, and looked it over. At once his eye caught the words, "The seventh day Saturday is the true Sabbath of the Bible. It is the day on which all the people in the Bible rested, and is the day on which the people in the new earth will rest." He was interested. He sat right down and read it through.

"Hey!" he shouted to some of his sailors. "Where did this tract come from?"

"A fellow named Alipati gave it to us."

"It speaks of a church that keeps Saturday for the Sabbath. Have any of you ever heard of such a church?"

"Yes, the *Lotu Savasava*. Alipati says they have a church across the bay at Suva Vou."

When the supplies were all loaded, Epenisa sailed across the bay and came to the Seventh-day Adventist mission. He found Alipati. He met Misi Fulitoni. He saw the *Rarama* coming off the little hand press. He was mightily impressed. He bought two shillings' worth of *Singa ni Vakathengu*, and took a number of the *Rarama* also. "I want them for my friends on the Ra Coast," he said. "They ought to know about the Bible Sabbath too."

While resting a week or two in his house before starting his next trip, he studied through the tract and the papers with his wife, his son, and his daughter-in-law.

"I believe it's right," said Epenisa one day.

"So do I," said his son.

"We do too," said their wives. And right there these four began to keep the Sabbath.

Epenisa soon found that he had more to talk about than cloth and sugar and oil as he traded for copra. Although all he knew was what he had read in the tract and the *Rarama* papers, he preached all he knew for all he was worth. He came to the town of Nanukuloa where the Ra district chief lived and had his court house. "Ratu Joni Mandriwewe ["John Sourbread"]," he said pleasantly, "did you ever hear that Saturday, not Sunday, is the real Bible Sabbath?"

"No, I never did," answered Ratu Joni. "Who told you that?"

"Here, read it for yourself. It's all in the Bible," Epenisa replied, and handed him a tract.

"Where did you get this?"

"From the *Lotu Savasava* in Suva Vou."

"The *Lotu Savasava*? Never heard of it."

"Well you ought to read what they say. I have, and I and my family belong to the *Lotu Savasava* already."

"You do?"

"Yes."

"Bring me some more of these tracts when you come the next time," requested Ratu Joni. "I want my *buli* ["under"] chiefs to hear about this."

"I will," called Epenisa as he hurried on.

From village to village he went, trading, talking, and giving away tracts. He came at last to the little town of Nambukandra, ninety miles from Suva. "Ratu Meli Salambongi," he called, "have you ever heard that Saturday, not Sunday, is the true Bible Sabbath?" Ratu Meli was now one of the *buli* chiefs under Ratu Joni. He became interested at once.

"Bring me some more of these tracts when you come next time," he pleaded. "I want to give them to my friends."

"I will," shouted Epenisa as he hurried on.

The next time he was in Suva he went to the mission in Suva Vou and bought two more shillings' worth of the tract *Singa ni Vakathengu.* "My wife and I, and my son and his wife are all keeping the seventh-day Sabbath now," he announced joyfully.

"You are?" gasped Pastor Fulton in utter amazement.

"Yes, and we tell everybody that we belong to the *Lotu Savasava.*"

"You do?"

"Yes, and Ratu Joni and Ratu Meli are interested. And they want more tracts for their friends."

"They do?" John Fulton could hardly speak, he was so amazed at the power of his mighty God.

Captain Epenisa took back the new supply of tracts. On his next trip to Suva he brought back some more. And in the villages of the Ra Coast the news of the Bible Sabbath began to work like leaven. After a time Ratu Joni sent a delegation down to Suva Vou. "There are many of us who are interested in the Bible Sabbath," they said, "and we want you to come and visit with us and study with us."

John listened to their plea. "I'll do my best to find time to come," he assured them, and they went away happy. But where could John find time? There was the *Rarama* that must be kept coming off the press every month. There was the translation of

Great Controversy that must continue with all speed. There was a new church building being erected at the mission headquarters right there in Suva Vou, and there was the care of the churches that were already established. So three months went by and the call could not be answered.

A second delegation was sent. The plea was even more urgent. Pastor Fulton gave them the same promise. But another three months went by and still John had not found time to visit the Ra Coast.

Then came a third delegation, headed by none other than Ratu Meli Salambongi himself. He was a large, well-built, pleasant-looking young man. He had a smile on his face and a cord in his hand. He introduced himself and then said, "Misi Fulitoni, we have sent two delegations asking you to come and visit us and preach to us, but you didn't come. Now Ratu Joni has sent *me,* and now I am going to bind you, hands and feet, and take you with us." He then caught hold of John Fulton's hands and laughed.

John trembled from sheer joy, excitement, and amazement for a moment, then said, "All right, my good brethren. I'll come with you. The work of God is so great that if I don't go now I may never find time." So John put them all in the *Thina,* and sailed around to the Ra Coast, and preached to them there for two or three weeks. And as time went on, he went again and again, till ultimately three new churches were organized there.

By this time the Parkers had been in Fiji about two years and Calvin was able to preach pretty well in Fijian, so that in between the times he worked as printer's devil helping to get out the *Rarama,* he and Pauliasi and Alipati were out in the villages preaching and distributing our literature. Some of his trips kept him away from home two or three weeks at a time and when he got back he couldn't help noticing that his good wife, Myrtle, was looking more and more run down.

9

"What can be the matter, my dear?" he asked. "You seem to have no appetite, and you are getting so pale and thin."

"Susie tells me it's just the enervating climate," she replied. "She says that all the wives of the government officials have a furlough every two years!"

Calvin thought a moment, then said, "The Coles had to have a change of climate after two years. So did the Fultons. Maybe we should ask Pastor Daniells what we should do." They did ask, and soon a letter came from Pastor Daniells inviting them to attend the union conference session in Australia. They went, and at that session were invited to assist in evangelistic work in Tasmania. So the Parkers got their change of climate after two years also.

"I don't know what I will do without you," said John as he said good-by.

"But we'll be back again soon," said Calvin with conviction. And sure enough, in time the Parkers did come back to dear old Fiji.

However, their departure left John Fulton alone once more. Alone? Oh no, not exactly. Edith was able to assume more and more responsibility for the *Rarama*. Besides, he had Susie and Jessie and Aganisi and Georgie, yes, and dear old Ratu Ambrose, and Pauliasi and Alipati and Tevita, and he had someone else too—a mighty God, able to do amazing things.

Every Man According
to His Ability

SOMETIMES WE MAY THINK that the only way the gospel can be preached is by ordained ministers holding formal evangelistic meetings. But when we do, we overlook the fact, which Paul emphasizes, that God can use foolish things, weak things, despised things, and even unseen things to perform His work. We would do well to remember that when the gifts of evangelists, apostles, and prophets were given to the church, so also was given the gift of helps (1 Cor. 12:28). And that it is when the possessors of these gifts have used them *according to their ability* (Acts 11:29) that the Lord's work has prospered. And that is why the Lord's work prospered in Fiji—because every man helped according to his ability. Listen to this:

Not long after Ratu Meli was baptized, an atheist trader came on business to his town. He claimed to be a wise man, and was soon making fun of the Fijian Christians and their Bible. "I don't believe in your Bible. I don't believe in your God. In fact, I don't believe in religion at all," he scoffed. "And see how successful I am! How wise I am!"

Now, Ratu Meli was not an ordained minister but he was one of God's helps. And under the inspiration of the Spirit of

Ratu Meli with a war club in one hand and a Bible in the other.

God, he looked the atheist square in the eye, and said, "Mr. Wiseman, our fathers used to believe just like you do. They didn't believe in the Bible or in God." Then pointing to an old stone oven nearby, he added, "Do you see that old stone oven over there? That is where they used to bake men before eating them. And if it weren't for the Bible and the gospel of Christ, we would still believe what you say you believe, and most likely by this time you would be in that oven being baked like a *vuaka mbalavu* for a feast. It's a good thing for you that *we* don't believe what *you* believe!"

And that man's wisdom was brought to naught. Maybe an ordained minister would have used some other argument, but according to his ability Ratu Meli just did his best, and God's work prospered.

Listen again. Remember Pauliasi Bunoa? He was a wonderful scholar, a seminary graduate, an indispensable translator, and yet withal a simple Fijian at heart. On one occasion just after he had made his decision to join the *Lotu Savasava,* he was coming to Sabbath school with his wife and three lovely daughters. As he left his house, some of the angry village folk followed along part of the way calling them names. Then before reaching the Sabbath school, rain came pelting down and they were soon soaked to the skin.

"Never mind, never mind," said Susie and Myrtle together. "We will lend you some of our clothes, while we hang yours up to dry."

"And you come in here, Pauliasi," said John Fulton, "and I'll soon have you looking like Misi Pauliasi." And John dressed him up in a set of underclothes and a long-tailed preacher's suit. They looked fine, and were greatly impressed with themselves all dressed up like Europeans. It made them happy, and they created quite a stir in the village as they returned home in these foreign clothes. The next day Pauliasi came to translate but he didn't bring back the clothes. A week went by, two weeks, but no clothes came back. Then John looked at Susie, and Susie looked at John. "Do you remember what Edward Hare told us about a Fijian loan being a gift?" she asked.

"I remember *now*," said John, "and this proves it. Next time I must remember a little sooner not to lend something I really need."

Yes, Pauliasi had his Fijian ways, but with them he had the Fijian ability to see and hear, which far exceeded the ability of the foreign missionaries. In addition to being the mission translator, Pauliasi acted as captain of the mission yacht, the *Thina*, and he was quite expert in finding the way around Viti Levu, Vanua Levu, and their many neighboring islands. On one occasion, however, John Fulton wanted to visit some of the more distant islands, so Pauliasi suggested that they hire an experienced pilot for the trip. All went well for a time. The pilot was a good navigator and guided them safely from island to island.

One day, however, when they were in mid-ocean, the wind died down and their boat stopped dead in the water. All afternoon and far into the night they waited for a breeze. About midnight the wind suddenly freshened. They set their course and were on their way again. In a few hours they could hear the distant moan of the waves dashing on the reef, and they knew they were approaching their destination. They knew where they were, but they also knew that the island was surrounded by a dangerous reef, and that there was only one opening through that reef into the harbor. But it was dark, and no one could see that entrance.

They came closer and closer. The moan of the waves increased to a roar. The pilot became uneasy and nervous. "I can't tell where the entrance is," he admitted. "I don't know what to do! I'm afraid we will be dashed to pieces on the reef."

"Pauliasi," called John Fulton, "I think you had better take charge. Stand up there in the bow and see if *you* can find the entrance."

At this point it seemed that each of the five Fijians on board had an idea of his own as to where the entrance was. And one shouted one thing and another shouted something else. But Pauliasi took charge at once and shouted "Silence!" They quieted down immediately and he continued, "It's too dark to *see* anything but a faint skyline above the mountains, and that won't do us any good. We will have to find the entrance by *sound*. Now, not one word from anyone!"

He then changed the course of the ship and ran her along parallel with the reef, and listened, hoping to hear a quiet place between the two points of the reef that marked the entrance. The others, realizing what he was doing, held their breath and also listened for all they were worth. After sailing some distance Pauliasi thought he detected a slight gap in the roaring of the waves, and ordered the pilot to reverse their direction and sail back again, this time a little closer to the reef. Back and forth for several times the *Thina* sailed while Pauliasi listened. Each time the quiet place between the two entrance points of the reef became more and more distinct to him. At last Pauliasi ordered, "All right, steer to the left! Now!" The helmsman obeyed, and soon the *Thina* and all aboard were anchored safely in the calm waters of the lagoon. It was God who gave Pauliasi the gift of keen hearing, but it was Pauliasi who used that gift according to his ability, to the saving of the ship and its passengers. And many, many times on many occasions Pauliasi did the same thing.

Now listen again. Do you remember Mr. Scott, the government officer, saying the officials were keeping their eyes on old Ratu Ambrose? Well, they did keep their eyes on him, and toward the end of 1901 they were so satisfied that Ratu

Ambrose was a new man, that they reappointed him to government service. It was now his business to visit the various chiefs
and to attend the various council meetings as the government
representative. Well Ratu Ambrose decided that if John Fulton
could accompany him to some of these councils it would give
him an opportunity to get acquainted with many of the re-
sponsible men in Fiji, and it would also give him an opportunity to preach to them. So he frequently urged John Fulton
to come with him.

One day he said, "Misi Fulitoni, there is to be a large land
council over on Mbengga just twenty miles away. If you will
come with me, you can hold a meeting with the many chiefs
who will be there."

"How do you know I will be able to preach?" questioned
John. "Won't they be too busy with their council work?"

"It will be all right," assured Ratu Ambrose. "I know all
those chiefs, and I know I can arrange it."

So they went over to the council meeting at Mbengga. The
chiefs were having a big time. After a while they stopped for a
recess, then Ratu Ambrose stood up and said, "Misi Fulitoni,
the *Lotu Savasava* preacher, is here this morning. Don't you
want to have a sermon?"

Several of them called out, *"Vinaka, vinaka!"* So after the
recess, John preached. When the sermon was finished, Ratu
Ambrose said, "Now, here is the preacher, ask him any Bible
question you wish, and he can give you the answer." One or
two questions were asked, but they were not to the point enough
to satisfy Ambrose, so he called out, "Tell them about Mrs.
White, Misi Fulitoni!"

John was a little embarrassed. He did not feel it was wise
to tell about Mrs. White in the first sermon, so he went on
talking about something else.

"But you haven't told them about Mrs. White yet," interrupted Ratu Ambrose. Fearing John might still hesitate, he stood up, faced the circle of chiefs, and said, "Have *you* got any prophet in *your* church? Have you? You know that in Old Testament times there were prophets in their churches, there were prophets in the New Testament churches, and the Bible says there will be prophets in the true church in the last days. Well the *Lotu Savasava* has a prophet. Yes, we do! And you all ought to belong to this church that has a prophet."

It was a short sermon, but it was another case of one who had the gift of helping to do what he could with all of his ability. And it certainly did no harm, for many of those chiefs went back to their homes and later welcomed into their midst the workers from the *Lotu Savasava*—the church that has a prophet.

I believe that the expression "every man" used in the title of this chapter includes the children also, and this is how the children helped in the preaching of the gospel according to their ability.

Listen. With the coming of the Parkers to Fiji an almost formal church school was formed. There were the two Fulton girls, Jessie and Agnes, with little baby brother Georgie to play around and generally get in the way, and the Parkers' daughter, Ramona, to begin with. Edith taught them every morning from about nine o'clock to twelve noon. However, after the little printing press came and the *Rarama* was started, Edith put in nearly full time at the press, so Myrtle Parker and Susie Fulton took over the teaching. Soon Pauliasi's two daughters, Miliana and Eseta, and Tevita's daughter, Liviana, joined the group of pupils and that made six. In the village there was a little boy named Nafitalai who had taken a great liking to little Georgie. He was about three years older than Georgie, and to keep him quiet in school Nafitalai came to school, and that made seven.

Just a few months after the press was set up, the mission families at Suva Vou were delighted to have a two-month visit from Pastor and Mrs. E. H. Gates. Now you may remember that Pastor and Mrs. Gates had come out on the mission ship *Pitcairn's* first voyage in 1890, and had settled for a time on Pitcairn Island. After baptizing eighty-two of the islanders and organizing the church there, he was asked by the General Conference to hold meetings and sell books in several of the other South Sea Islands, with a view to finding openings for permanent workers to settle there. He even spent some time with John I. Tay in Fiji in 1890, holding meetings and selling books in a number of the islands. In 1892 he paid another visit to Pitcairn, and at this time established their school. In 1894 he returned to the United States. But the South Sea Islands were continually on his heart and in 1899 he and his good wife came to Pitcairn once more on the sixth and last voyage of our mission ship. The islanders rejoiced greatly to have them in their midst again, and now after being there for some time, they came on their second visit to Fiji.

While the men busied themselves preaching the gospel and visiting the people to whom Pastor Gates had sold books during his first visit to Fiji, Mrs. Gates felt the burden of enlarging the church school. Didn't they have a lovely new church? Why couldn't they hold school in it during the week? She soon had Susie and Pauliasi quite enthusiastic about it. They both promised to help as they could, and soon there were about two dozen boys and girls from seven to twelve years of age in our Suva Vou church school. A lovely Fijian girl about sixteen years of age named Nancy was hired by Susie Fulton to help with the housework so that she could assist with the teaching.

Mrs. Gates proved to be an excellent organizer and a strict disciplinarian and succeeded in convincing the students that,

since they belonged to the *Lotu Savasava,* it was their business
to let their light shine. And this spirit continued with the children long after the Gateses had gone on to Australia.

For a few moments let us take a peek at some of these
little folks while they were at play after school early in 1902.
Jessie was then nine and a half, Aganisi eight, Georgie almost
five, Georgie's friend Nafitalai eight, Miliana eleven, Eseta ten,
and Liviana also ten. Never mind the others just now. These
little ones being children of the workers and church officers
usually played together.

"Let's go down to the beach and scare the crabs into their
holes," said Aganisi one afternoon.

"Oh, yes! Oh, yes!" chorused the others, and off to the
beach they ran. As they stamped their feet on the wet sand
thousands of little crabs scrambled sideways into their holes.
The children laughed with glee.

"Hey! What's that?" asked Georgie pointing excitedly to
two big lumps on the sand not far away.

Nafitalai looked and said, "Turtles! Two turtles! Someone
has caught them and turned them over on their backs so they
can't run away!"

"O-o-o-oh! Somebody is going to cook them for a feast!"
said Liviana.

"But turtles are not clean," declared Jessie stoutly. "They
don't have scales! They are just great big shellfish."

"Yes, and even if you call them animals, they sure don't
chew the cud or part the hoof," added Miliana with a feeling
of superior wisdom.

"Yes," declared Aganisi indignantly, "and they shouldn't
eat unclean things. What say we turn them over and let them
run away into the ocean again. That would be letting our
light shine, wouldn't it?"

"Oh, yes!" said Georgie.

"Oh, yes!" said Miliana. But Nafitalai and Eseta and Liviana weren't quite so sure.

"But somebody might get mad at us," cautioned Liviana.

"I don't care if they do!" declared Jessie. "Come on, who will help me turn them over?"

"I will, I will," said Georgie and Aganisi and Miliana all together. They turned them over, and the two huge turtles joyfully lumbered back to the water and disappeared into the depths of the ocean.

Now, I don't intend to argue whether they did right or wrong, but *they* thought they were letting their light shine according to their ability, and you will have to admit there was at least one less feast of unclean food in Fiji because of what they did.

"I know! I know!" cried Jessie one other afternoon after school. "Let's play funerals!"

"Oh, yes! Oh, yes!" chorused the members of the children's clique.

"But what shall we bury?" asked Aganisi.

"I know where there is a dead bird," said Eseta.

"Goody! Goody!" chorused the others.

"Then you get the dead bird, Eseta," ordered Jessie. "I'll get a shoe box from the house for a coffin. And, Nafitalai, you and Georgie dig the grave."

"Where?" asked Nafitalai with excitement.

"Under this mango tree will do," said Jessie, and she flew to the house for the shoe box while Eseta rushed off to find the dead bird. When all was ready, Jessie took command. "The procession will form at the house," she said. "I'll be the preacher and I will lead. Georgie and Nafitalai can be the pall-bearers, then you girls can be the mourners and follow the coffin."

It was all very solemn and impressive. The procession

formed, the "preacher" led the way to the graveside. They sang "Jesus Loves Me," "When He Cometh," and "Lift Up the Trumpet." On the inspiration of the moment Jessie preached about the two sparrows that were sold for a farthing, yet God noticed when even one of them died. "And you must all remember," she declared solemnly, "nobody goes to heaven when he dies. The dead just sleep in the grave till the resurrection." Then she asked Eseta to pray.

"No! No!" whispered Eseta. "It's my bird. I'm the chief mourner."

"Oh, so you are. I forgot about that," admitted Jessie. "Then, Aganisi, you pray."

So Aganisi prayed. The coffin was lowered into the grave, and the dirt was filled in. For a moment there was awed silence, then—"Flowers!" gasped Aganisi. "No one brought any flowers! Why didn't we think of flowers? You can't have a funeral without flowers. Come on, Eseta." And the two scampered off to get some flowers from Mother Fulton's prized garden.

"And the tombstone!" gasped Nafitalai. "Graves have to have tombstones!"

"Yes, but where——"

"I know where there are some flat pieces of soapstone," shouted Nafitalai as he took to his heels, "and it is soft enough so I can cut the name with my knife."

"Good!" shouted the delighted mourners. And before too long the grave was bedecked with flowers and an imposing tombstone, which bore the name "Pretty Bird" at the head. The children ohed and ahed, and the funeral was over.

"I like playing funerals," said Georgie.

"So do I. So do I," agreed each one of the group.

"Let's play funerals again tomorrow," suggested Liviana.

"Oh, yes. Let's do!" they all agreed! So with their eyes

shining in anticipation they gathered at the mango tree after
school the next day.

"What have we got to bury today?" asked Jessie.

Everyone looked around and listened, but no one spoke.

"Couldn't you find a single dead thing we could bury?"
asked Jessie.

"Nothing! Couldn't find a thing!" was the general reply.

"Well, I found a beetle," said Nafitalai. "Would that do?
It's a *vaka levu sara* ["very big one"]."

"Yes, that will do," replied Jessie. And they buried that
beetle with more honor and ceremony than any of its ancestors
ever knew or heard tell of.

The next day one of the girls had found a dead mouse and
again a coffin was found, the grave dug, and the procession
formed.

But the next day they were stuck. Not one of them could
find a single thing that could be buried. There was an air of
dejection and sadness that none of their other funerals had
ever had, till suddenly Aganisi's eyes lighted up. "I know!" she
fairly shouted. "Jessie, let's bury our dolls!"

"Your dolls!" exclaimed three horrified little girls in unison.
"How could you?"

"Yes, but," beamed Aganisi, "we could bury them just for
today, then tomorrow we could have a resurrection!"

"A resurrection?" asked all of the little girls plus the two
little boys as their eyes bugged out and their eyebrows lifted
while the idea sank in. Then suddenly they danced up and
down, and clapped their hands. "Yes! Yes!" they cried. "Let's
bury the dolls today and have a resurrection tomorrow." So they
did. That is, they had the funeral part, with more singing and
praying and weeping than they had ever had before.

But that night Aganisi couldn't go to sleep. "What's the
matter, dear?" Mother Fulton inquired kindly.

"Nothing," replied Aganisi shutting her eyes tight. But there was something the matter, and although she wouldn't tell, her little heart felt very much as though there had been a real death in her family. Her arms were empty. She wondered if the white ants or the mice or the———. She shuddered at the awful, haunting thoughts. Suddenly, the lightning flashed, the thunder roared, and it began to rain. Jessie was out of bed in a second. "Aganisi," she whispered. "I can't sleep."

"Neither can I," confided Aganisi.

"Do you think they will get wet?"

"I'm sure they will."

"Don't you think we ought to have the resurrection now?"

"But how could we? It's raining."

"Yes, but father would help us."

"Do you think he would? At midnight?"

"I'm sure he would. Come on, let's ask him."

Two tearful girls crept over to their great big father and poured out their heartbroken tale of woe.

"Of course I'll help you," he answered with a big smile. They put on their raincoats. John Fulton got the spade. They went to the foot of the old mango tree, and there at midnight, in the rain, they had their resurrection, and within minutes two happy little girls were sound asleep with their resurrected dollies in their arms.

"I don't want to play funerals anymore," confided Jessie to the members of the clique the next day after school.

"Me neither!" said Aganisi solemnly.

"Well, I know!" said Nafitalai.

"What?" demanded the group.

"Let's play preaching. Jessie can be Pastor Gates and preach in English and Liviana can translate into Fijian."

"Oh, yes! Oh, yes!" they all agreed. And once more their eyes sparkled.

"All right then, sit down," commanded Jessie. And they sang, and preached, and translated, and listened, exactly as they had seen done in many a meeting. It even ended in an appeal for all who wanted to join the *Lotu Savasava* to stand up. And everyone stood.

"Jessie," suggested Miliana, "now you ought to take us down to the little river and baptize us."

"Oh, yes! Oh, yes!" cried the rest of the children with delight. And baptized they were. Jessie led them down to the river and baptized them all.

Now, of course, I don't intend to argue that this was the right kind of game to play. I will only say that subsequent chapters will reveal a little of the influence of these childish games that were played in all innocency according to their ability.

About this time John and Susie Fulton recognized that Jessie was getting too old to continue in school on Fiji.

"Whatever are we going to do?" sighed Susie.

"I'm sure I don't know," John replied. "She's getting too big to stay here in Fiji. She needs to be in school with children her own age."

"Where could we send her? America is too far away."

"Well, what about Australia?"

"You mean, send her to Avondale College?"

"Why not?"

"Well, let us think about it," said John. And they did think about it.

At Avondale

AS THE YEAR 1901 drew near to its close, John Fulton became more and more conscious of the need for better transportation among the islands. In the *Thina* they were dependent on the winds, and were at the mercy of the storms and the waves. There was no telling when they might be becalmed or when they might have to spend the night in the open sea waiting for a safe entrance to some harbor. There was no question about it, they needed a motor launch. This would make them independent of the capricious winds, and enable them to plan and keep their appointments with greater certainty.

The more John thought about it, the more enthusiastic he became about it. He talked about it to everyone he met. He mentioned it in every letter he wrote, and the Australian *Union Conference Record* of February, 1902 published an article in which he said:

If your hearts are in the work for the island people, send in some money to help this work along. General Booth of the Salvation Army used to say, "It would be foolish to try to save a shipwrecked crew by having a fine choir stand on the beach and sing 'Rescue the perishing, care for the dying.'" So it would be vain for us to only sing and pray about preaching the third angel's message. We must also *give,* that some of us can *go.* A short time ago it was reported that we Seventh-day Adventists were giving less than one half penny [one cent U.S. at the time] per week per member for missions. Why, my dear people, if you would just give the value of the eggs laid by one good missionary hen each week to missions, you could be giving ten or fifteen times that amount. And then if you fed that missionary hen plenty of wheat and other good things, you could do better still. Why not dedicate a hen or two to missions! The cackle of such fowls would be much more cheering to your toiling missionaries than mere song and prayers with no "give" in them. I am glad the Sabbath school offerings for the first quarter of 1902 have been dedicated to the work in Fiji, to give us a much-needed motor launch. It will take all you can do, and all you can give.

The article did more than make people smile. It touched their hearts, and the donations began to roll in. Of course, you can realize that it would take time for the money to come in, and time for the launch to be built, but in this waiting time John and Susie had something else to think about, and something else to make them happy. A letter from G. A. Irwin, president of the Australasian Union Conference at the time, told of the appointment of Arthur Currow and his family to join the mission staff in Fiji. The letter said he would be arriving soon.

This news was most encouraging, and they began to make plans for their arrival right away. However, this good news did not solve the problem of Jessie's schooling. They were still giving serious thought to that. No wonder, then, that one day Susie said to John, "You know, the school year at Avondale has already opened. But I do not think we should wait till next year to send Jessie over. I wish we could find someone to send her with soon."

Then Edith surprised them both by saying, "Why couldn't I take her over? You know, I've been thinking lately that I ought to go to Avondale to finish my education too."

"Why, Edith!" said Susie. "Since when have you been thinking about going to Avondale?"

"Ever since you began thinking about sending Jessie over,"

she replied. "You know I will be twenty years old soon, and—"
the color rushed into her cheeks as she added, "and you know—I
might——"

"You might what?"

"Well, you know, I might——"

"Of course, I know," chuckled Susie, as if she had just
thought of it for the first time. "You might be able to recruit a
young man missionary for Fiji."

Edith put her arm around Susie, laid her head on her shoulder, and whispered, "You are such an understanding little
mother."

Immediately John and Susie gave some more serious thought
to the matter, with the result that Edith and Jessie were on the
May boat, on their way to Avondale. Edith at twenty years of
age was a capable young woman, and Jessie had her tenth
birthday, May 24, during the voyage.

After this things began to happen rapidly. Hardly had John
and Susie said good-by to Edith and Jessie, when Arthur Currow
and his family arrived and settled down in the Parkers' house
in Suva Vou. And hardly had the Currows settled down when a
letter arrived saying the Parkers would soon be on their way back
to Fiji.

"Things are beginning to look up for Fiji at last," John remarked to Susie. "I'm sure that when Calvin gets here he will
want to open up work on one of the other islands."

"Yes," said Susie, "and next we will be needing a training
school."

"But before that I must get *Great Controversy* in Fijian
printed," interjected John. "Pauliasi's translation is just about
finished; then we must get some colporteurs started selling our
books."

Almost while they were talking a young man knocked on
their door.

"Do you remember me, *Turanga* ["Master"]?" he asked.

"I don't think I do," replied John.

"My name is Samuela. I live in the mountains, in the Tholo district."

"Yes?"

"Two years ago, when you were living in Tamavua, three other young men and I slept in your house one night."

"I'm beginning to remember a little," said John. "And———"

"And the *Marama* fed us some of her homemade bread. We had never tasted anything so delicious in all our lives before."

"Yes, and———"

"That night we must have been too excited, for we had never seen the ocean before, and as we tossed around we kicked the leg off the stove."

"Yes, now I remember," said John.

"But you weren't angry with us. And the *Marama* told us the story about Daniel interpreting Nebuchadnezzar's dream. And she showed us a picture of the image. I've never forgotten it."

John put his hand on the young man's shoulder and said, "Samuela, come with me and let me show you something." And he took him over to the pressroom where the boys were turning out the next edition of the *Rarama.* Samuela's eyes widened. "The *Rarama!*" he said. But before he could say any more, John placed the little book of Bible studies in his hands opened to the picture of the image of Daniel two.

"Oh! Oh! Oh! That's it!" exclaimed Samuela. "And it is in our language! I want it, and I want some *Raramas* to take to my brother Methusela ["Methuselah"] who is a teacher in the Tholo district." Then looking earnestly into John's face, Samuela added, "I wish the *Lotu Savasava* had a training school where some of us young men could come and prepare to be preachers. I would love to be able to preach about that image of Daniel two."

John gave him a supply of *Raramas* and a few copies of the small book of Bible studies, and as he left, John said to himself, "School! A training school for preachers! I expect to hear from Samuela again someday."

By June, the Parkers had arrived, and as John had already guessed, Calvin was all excited about opening up work on a new island. "I would like to try to find a location on one of the islands in the Lau group," he said. "You know the first missionaries landed over there in Lakemba, and there must be a lot of Christians over that way." So John, Calvin, and Pauliasi went aboard the *Thina* and went cruising around. Before long Calvin said, "I like the look of the little town of Loma Loma on the island of Vanua Mbalavu. It is near Lakemba, and I wouldn't be treading on anyone's toes there."

"*Vinaka, Vinaka!*" said Pauliasi.

"And we can arrange to have Pauliasi work with you sometimes," said John. "Our translation of *Great Controversy* is just about finished."

"*Vinaka, Vinaka!*" said Calvin.

In a month or so the Parkers were settled in a temporary Fijian house in Loma Loma on the island of Vanua Mbalavu.

"As you visit around, Calvin," said John earnestly, "keep your eyes open for a plantation that could be bought, which is centrally located where we could establish a training school, because that's the next big thing on our program after we get the colporteurs out selling *Great Controversy*."

"I certainly will," replied Calvin.

Before too long Calvin purchased a yacht, a little smaller than the *Thina.* He named it the *Ramona* after his six-year-old daughter. He was thus enabled to travel extensively and conveniently around the islands.

In a few months Calvin sailed over to Suva Vou just to see how things were progressing at headquarters.

"Everything is going along splendidly," said John, "and God has helped us overcome quite a serious problem. But first let me tell you how proud I am of our Fijian Adventist men."

"Proceed," urged Calvin. "I always like to hear of the faithfulness of our Fijians."

"Well, a few weeks ago an order was given through the village chiefs for all the men to cut a certain quantity of poles and bamboos, and float them across the bay to Suva, where they were to be built into temporary booths to accommodate some visiting officials."

"Yes?"

"Well, our men cut their poles, and finished tying them into a raft just before sunset Friday evening."

"Yes?"

"Of course, the other village men took their rafts across the bay on Sabbath. But our men did not. Our men went to church and waited till the sun set on Sabbath and then took their raft over at night."

"Did they get into trouble?"

"Of course! 'What's the matter with you *Lotu Savasava* men?' growled the officers when they turned up. 'Why didn't you get here with your raft when the other men did?' And Calvin, what do you think? Instead of saying their missionaries told them not to work on Sabbath, they humbly opened the Bible to the fourth commandment and read it to the officers. Then they said, 'Sirs, we feel we should obey God first.' The officers were a bit surprised, but were evidently quite satisfied and said no more."

"Splendid!" responded Calvin fervently. "I knew our Fijians would be faithful. And now, John, what was the problem?"

"Well, you know, Calvin, the government has felt that only the Methodists, the Wesleyans, and the Roman Catholics should be permitted to do missionary work in these islands. Recently the Mormons applied for permission to work here and were refused. But when we first came we didn't know that we had to get permission to work, so we just went right ahead and soon had a constituency, and, of course, that gave us a right to stay. The fact is, however, the government regards us as nonconformists and has repeatedly denied us the privilege of being registered so that we could perform legal marriages. So when our young people get married, we can only give them the religious part of the service and then they have to go before a civil magistrate to do the legal part."

"Yes, I know."

"I wrote to the government officials, but back came the reply, 'His Excellency does not see his way clear to grant your request.' I wrote again. But my request was not granted."

"So?"

"Well, one day not long ago I was walking past a lawyer's office in town. The lawyer saw me and called, 'Come in for a moment, Misi Fulitoni.' I went in and he said, 'Is it true that you have been denied the privilege of being registered to perform legal marriages?' 'Yes,' I replied, 'it is true.' Then he asked, 'Are the Adventist ministers denied this privilege in any other British country?' 'None that I know of,' I replied. 'Then, look, Misi Fulitoni,' said the lawyer. 'My brother is the chief justice of Fiji. Write another request immediately, saying you have had legal advice, and see what happens.'"

"And?"

"And I did. And, Calvin, in a very short time I received a large book of certificates and a letter saying I had been duly registered."

"That's wonderful!" rejoiced Calvin.

"And I advise you to do the same, Calvin, so that you can be registered also. Then we can both do all that is necessary for our own young people."

"I certainly will," said Calvin. Within a short time he also was registered.

Before Calvin returned to Loma Loma, he and John spoke of many things in connection with the work, and they were soon discussing the Fijian *Great Controversy*. "Say, John," said Calvin, "are you going to attempt printing *Great Controversy* on the little hand press?"

"No! No! It's too big a job for that."

"And it's too far to send it to the Pacific Press in Oakland."

"Yes, I've been thinking about sending it to the Bible Echo Press in Melbourne, or the college press in Avondale, maybe."

"Avondale? That's right, the school was opened eight years ago and last year as soon as Elder Gates arrived in Australia he began to establish a printing press in a corner of the health food factory, so by now they must have a fairly good print shop, where they teach the students printing."

"And I even began to think that it would pay *me* to go over and look after the printing and proofreading myself."

"I believe it would pay in every way," agreed Calvin. "Look at the time it would save. And Edith could set the type! And say, you could print the *Rarama* while you were all there also."

"Yes, and we could be with Jessie, too."

"Susie would not object to that."

"Indeed she would not, Calvin. And between you and me, Susie and I have both been feeling under the weather for some time lately, and I think a change of climate for a while will do us a world of good."

Calvin sailed back to Loma Loma in his little yacht the *Ramona*. And John thought some more about the advisability of going to Avondale to print the Fijian *Great Controversy*. But he did more than think about it. He wrote to the brethren in Australia and in America, asking their advice. Soon the letters

Top: Bird's-eye view of old Australasian Missionary College, Cooranbong, New South Wales.

Middle: Bird's-eye view of Avondale College, successor to Australasian Missionary College.

Bottom: The Ellen G. White Memorial building at Avondale College.

came back giving hearty approval to his suggestion, and the letter from Australia added, "And in your spare time in between printing the *Great Controversy* and the Fijian periodical the *Rarama,* we would like you to teach Bible in the Avondale College."

So it happened that by the end of 1902 John and Susie with their three children were nicely settled in a little cottage half-way between Coorangbong village church and Avondale College. By this time enough money had come in so that an order for the new motor launch could be placed with a good boat-builder in Suva, and Arthur Currow was there on the spot to supervise the building of it.

John set to work with a will printing *Great Controversy* and the *Rarama.* Edith supervised setting the type, and Susie helped with the proofreading. Fortunately, about this time a nineteen-year-old young woman, Eva Edwards, came to Avondale. She needed work to help put herself through school, so she gladly joined the Fulton family as general assistant, and thus made it possible for Susie to spend more time in the printing business.

By the time school opened in 1903 there was little spare time but John stretched himself to his utmost and made time in which to teach Bible in the college. He did more than that. He conceived the idea of printing a devotional calendar. It had twelve pages for the twelve months of the year. In addition to the calendar for each month, there was a short Bible study on each page, giving verses of Scripture about the Creation, the Sabbath, the fall of man, the nature of man, the promise of a Saviour, Christ's first coming, signs of His second coming, and our promised home in heaven. He thought that such a calendar would be kept on the walls of the Fijian homes, and would bear daily witness to the truth. And that little calendar certainly did.

But John did more than print *Great Controversy*, the *Rarama*, the calendar, and teach Bible in the college. He attended committee meetings, preached in churches and at camp meetings, and wherever he had the opportunity he told about Fiji and how the light of truth was beginning to dispel the darkness. He told of Ratu Ambrose, of Pauliasi, of Alipati, of Ratu Joni, and Ratu Meli. He told of being becalmed in the ocean and how Pauliasi found the entrance through the reef by his keen hearing. He told of their need for the new motor launch. He told of the crying need of a worker to open up work among the Indians, who were about as numerous as the Fijians. He told of the need of a training school for Fiji's young men. Everywhere he went he talked Fiji. He was so full of Fiji that when he preached, the people smiled and said, "Pastor 'Fiji' is going to talk today." But people did more than smile. His enthusiasm inspired them too.

"We must see that he gets an engine for his motor launch," said one of the union committee members.

"Yes, and find a young man to put in charge of the training school," added another.

Louis Currow, the brother of Arthur Currow who had recently settled in Fiji, said, "Brethren, I'd be glad to volunteer for self-supporting work among the Indians in Fiji. Arthur says he thinks a treatment room in Suva would be quite successful."

"I would like to volunteer too," said Eva Edwards. "Aren't there some things that only a woman worker can do for the Indian women?"

"And I would like to be a teacher in Fiji," said Sybil Reed who was graduating from Avondale that year.

"And," added Edith a little shyly, "I know a young man who would make a very good school man."

"Who is he?" asked John.

"His name is Mr. Carr."

"Septimus Carr?"

"Yes."

"But how do you know he would be willing to go to Fiji?"
Edith blushed her prettiest as she replied, "He told me."

The good brethren did more than talk. Letters crossed the
Pacific to the General Conference containing requests and pro-
posals, with the result that in September of 1903, Louis Currow,
and his wife and two children, George and Miriam, with Eva
Edwards set sail for Fiji to open up a treatment room in Suva,
and on the same boat with them was Sybil Reed who was going
to join the Parkers at Loma Loma. In addition to all this, an
order was placed with a company in California to ship at once
an engine for the motor launch.

By this time the printing part of the Fijian *Great Controversy* was about finished, so the next month Susie Fulton,
with Agnes, Georgie, and Edith, returned to Suva Vou, leaving
Jessie to finish out the school year, and John to await the binding of his precious book.

Septimus Carr had another school year to go before he could
leave, but he joined John Fulton as his special assistant and
began learning Fijian right away. Septimus had one more source
of learning and inspiration. As chief assistant to John he was
privileged to sort out all the Fulton mail. Jessie could not help
noticing that every time there was mail from Fiji, Septimus took
possession of one letter plainly marked "Pastor J. E. Fulton."

"But that's got my father's name on it," objected Jessie.

"Yes, but can't you read the words in the corner of the
envelope?" he replied.

And Jessie read, *"Ngginggi ni vanua."*

Then they both laughed, for that is Fijian for "chariot."

"You see! That letter is for me, 'Mr. Chariot.' It is from
Edith."

Septimus laughed at the clever idea. But eleven-year-old Jessie puckered up her brow and said, "But why does Edith send the *ngginggi ni vanua* letter to my father?"

Then Septimus laughed some more and said, "Someday, Jessie, you will be old enough to know how Cupid helps us find ways to be in love and still keep the school rules."

The weeks passed quickly, and before long school was out. The Fijian *Great Controversy* was bound and packed securely in boxes, and by the end of 1903 the Fultons were all together again in Suva Vou, with their new precious book.

It was soon decided that Eva Edwards was needed more in Suva Vou than in the Suva treatment rooms, so she became one of the family again.

When the Fultons arrived in Suva Vou, the engine for the new mission motor launch already had arrived and had been installed, so everybody was ready for a new chapter of the work in Fiji.

"What are you going to name the new launch?" asked Susie.

"We have already been calling her *Andi Suva* ["Queen of Suva"]," said the shipbuilder, "for she is the most beautiful launch and the most seaworthy that I have ever built."

"*Andi Suva*," said John thoughtfully. "That sounds good. *Andi Suva* it shall be till we decide on a better name."

But the name *Andi Suva* stuck.

The Great Controversy

THE NEW CHAPTER in the work for Fiji began with a bang! As soon as possible one of the boxes containing the new *Great Controversy* was opened. Alipati was on hand, and such ohing and ahing and dancing up and down and clapping of hands as you have never imagined took place.

"I must start selling them right now," said Alipati. And he did. Nothing could hold him back. He went all through Suva and Tamavua and the nearby villages and sold *Great Controversy* everywhere.

"Misi Fulitoni," he begged one day, "if you could only take me and a big box of books in the new launch to the Ra Coast, I'm sure I could sell a lot of books there."

"I will," said John, and to the Ra Coast they went. Left alone, Alipati did more than just sell books. He preached and talked the message and also health reform everywhere he went. He did more than just *talk* health reform. He had watched Mrs. Parker and Mrs. Fulton and Mrs. Gates while they performed wonders with fomentation cloths, sweat baths, and compresses, and now he took his turn at treating the sick with hydrotherapy. He knew how to improvise fomentation cloths by using a wet cloth and a hot water bag. He knew how to make a sweat bath with a Primus stove and a pan of water under a chair, while the patient was enveloped in a heavy blanket, and it wasn't long before the village folks found a new name for him. They called him Dr. Tanga ni Wai Kata-kata ("Dr. Hot Water Bag"). But God greatly blessed Alipati, and Dr. Hot Water Bag healed the sick and sold books.

After some time he returned with great joy to Suva Vou for more books. "Misi Fulitoni," he exclaimed, "what is the largest number of books you ever sold in one house?"

John thought a moment then replied, "I can remember once selling three books in one home."

"Three books?"

"Yes, three. Why? What is the largest number you have sold in one house?"

"Thirteen!" he exulted, and a halo of light seemed to glow around his face.

"Thirteen?" said John a little skeptically.

"Yes, thirteen!" said Alipati triumphantly, then hastened to explain. "You see I was in Ratu Joni's house in Nanukuloa and he was holding a council meeting with the subchiefs of his district. Of course, you know Ratu Joni is a member of the legislative assembly of the colony, and is therefore highly respected. Ratu Meli was also there, and can you believe it? Ratu Joni let me tell about the book *Great Controversy* before them all, and then *he* bought one and advised each one of them to buy a copy also. And they did!"

"Splendid!" said John.

"And now Ratu Joni wants you to come over and hold some meetings in his town."

"I will go, Alipati," John replied with emotion. "Truly health reform is the right arm of the message and our literature work and our colporteurs are the feet of the message. We must follow where they lead."

In due time John Fulton went over to Nanukuloa, Ratu Joni's town, and inquired for a place where he could hold some meetings.

"You are welcome to use the courthouse, Misi Fulitoni," said Ratu Joni. "During the last hurricane the Wesleyan church here was wrecked, so they have their services in the courthouse on Sunday, but you are welcome to use it any other time."

"Thank you, Ratu Joni," said John, "then I'll start tonight."

"Right above the table," added Ratu Joni, "the Wesleyans have hung a large kerosene lamp. Feel free to use it, Misi Fulitoni."

"Thank you, Ratu Joni, I will," replied John.

That evening the old *lali* that was once used to call people to a cannibal feast was beaten loud and long to call people to a gospel meeting, and a good number of people responded. The courthouse was filled. John went through the usual opening exercises and was well into his sermon, when the local Wesleyan preacher, dressed in his long white minister's gown, strode angrily into the courthouse and pushed his way right down to the table where John was standing.

"Do you wish to say something?" asked John quietly, hoping that nothing would happen to interrupt the meeting.

"Yes, I do," he shouted. Then pointing to the lamp he added, "That is our Wesleyan light."

John didn't want to have an argument so he replied, "I am sorry if our using it displeases you. But do what you think is best."

"I will," he said, and he reached up and extinguished the light. Then he strode outside again. At once several hand lanterns were lighted and passed up to the table, and John went on with his sermon.

Just then Ratu Joni entered the courthouse and sat down near the door. Noticing that the large hanging lamp was not burning, he whispered to the man beside him, "What's the matter with the big lamp?"

"The Wesleyan preacher came in and put it out," the man whispered back.

"He did?" said Ratu Joni indignantly. He rose suddenly and hurried down the path to the nearby parsonage and made no attempt to conceal his rage. "You ought to be ashamed of yourself," he shouted at the preacher. "Do you think you can put out the Adventist light by an act like this? The Adventist light comes from the Bible and you can never put it out. Look away up there in the mountains where the towns are many. You will see, the Adventists will go up there also and set up their light, and you will lose much. After the meeting tonight take your lamp and all your belongings out of the courthouse, and then find some other place to worship till your church is rebuilt."

But this was not the end of the controversy. The humbled preacher took his lamp out of the courthouse and then distributed D. M. Canright's book *Adventism Renounced* to all who could read English. He gave one copy to Ratu Joni who could read and speak English fluently. But in a few days he returned it saying, "I didn't like that book. I only read the preface. If it took Canright twenty-eight years to find out that he was wrong in keeping Sabbath with the Adventists, then he must have been a fool and I don't care to read what he says."

Little did John Fulton realize at the time how prophetic was Ratu Joni's statement about the Adventists setting up their light in the mountains, or how soon that prophecy would be fulfilled. You will remember the visit of Samuela in 1902, and how he took the little book of Bible studies and some copies of the *Rarama* back into the mountainous Tholo district for his brother Methusela to read. Well, Methusela was teaching a Wesleyan school up there, and he read and studied, and re-

11

read and restudied that little book and those papers for two
years. By the end of that time he had made up his mind that
he was going to keep the Sabbath. So he called the townspeople
together, and said, "Dear friends, I have been studying for two
years and I am convinced that the seventh day of the week is
the true Bible Sabbath, and I am going to keep it."

Angry voices were heard on every side. "Turncoat! That's
what you are," yelled some.

"Jew!" yelled others.

"Well, you can't teach my children anymore," called out
another.

"Nor mine!"

"Nor mine, either," said others.

Methusela had carefully weighed his decision and this was
just about what he had expected. So he said calmly, "Then if
you wish I will resign and you can call a new teacher."

However, not everyone in the town was against him.
Methusela still had many friends, and right then one of them
called out, "Well, if *you* don't want him to teach *your* children,
he can stay and teach *mine* anyway."

"Mine too."

"And mine too," shouted several others.

But Methusela said, "I will not stay unless you let me go
down to the coast and bring up an Adventist preacher. Then
after you have heard his explanation, if you want me to stay,
I'll stay."

"That's fair," shouted several.

"Yes, you go and bring up an Adventist preacher and let
us hear what he will say," agreed others. So Methusela set out
to go to the coast.

It was not many days before he found the *Lotu Savasava*
at Suva Vou, and there he found Alipati bubbling over with
enthusiasm over his success in selling *Great Controversy* in the

Ra Coast district. Alipati showed Methusela the new book in the Fijian language, and quickly sold him a copy. Methusela sat right down and read day and night till he had read it through.

"Alipati," he begged, "there are many people in the Tholo district who need this book. Please, please come back with me and bring a whole box of books." Then he told how he had been giving Bible studies for two years, but was still the only one keeping the Sabbath up in the mountains. He told how angry some of the townspeople were, and how he had promised to bring an Adventist preacher to explain the Bible to them. Then he added, "I am sure God wants *you* to come with me *now.*"

And so it came to pass that in a day or two John Fulton put a box of books in the launch, took Methusela and Alipati on board, sailed out of Suva harbor, turned north, entered the Rewa River, then branched off into the Wainimbuka River and went as far as the river would permit them toward the Tholo mountains. The Spirit of God took possession of Alipati. He began at once selling books, treating the sick, and preaching. He preached in the morning, he preached at noon, he preached at night. He was as Paul says, "Instant in season, out of season." His enthusiasm was infectious and soon the whole district was ablaze with the Adventist light. As the years went by, the light became brighter and brighter till there were three churches organized there. Thus was Ratu Joni's prophecy speedily fulfilled. God used Alipati to sow the seed that later produced a bountiful harvest and kindled a light that never went out.

The months from May to August, 1904, went serenely by, with the missionaries and faithful Alipati in Suva Vou printing the *Raramas,* preaching the gospel, and selling *Great Controversy* everywhere, while Brother and Sister Parker, Sybil Reed, and Pauliasi, situated at Loma Loma, were preaching the gospel and selling *Great Controversy* in the eastern islands.

But you couldn't expect Satan to sit idly by and not attempt in some way to destroy their work or drive them from it. The *Great Controversy* was more than just the name of a book. It was the name of a real struggle going on between the forces of good and evil, and in September, Satan put forth his hand and touched the life of little seven-year-old Georgie.

Georgie was a handsome little boy—the image of his father—and was loved by everybody old and young alike. He enjoyed the usual good health of most of the children in Fiji, with nothing more serious than an occasional cold or a slight attack of fever. Agnes remembers with a smile that on September 13 at morning worship his father was teaching him the memory verse for Sabbath: "I am with thee, and no man shall *set* on thee to hurt thee" (Acts 18:10). Georgie repeated it, "I am with thee, and no man shall *sit* on thee to hurt thee." Then in his childish innocence he wondered why the others smiled.

The first intimation they had of anything being the matter was September 15, when Eva Edwards was playing with the children in the back yard. She was trying to catch Georgie when all of a sudden he put out his hands and said, "Eva, don't chase me anymore. Chase the girls. I have a pain in my side." Still no one thought that a pain in his side meant anything serious. Maybe it was just a little stomach-ache. But stomach-ache or not, all the rest of that day and the next, Georgie was noticeably not well.

Sabbath morning, September 17, he was not hungry for breakfast. And they had rice and prunes for breakfast! They all knew that these were Georgie's favorite breakfast foods, so Father Fulton remarked, "Well, if Georgie doesn't want to have rice and prunes, he must be feeling pretty sick." Looking over to Mother Fulton, he added, "Susie, maybe he shouldn't go to Sabbath school this morning."

"I think you're right," said Susie. "I'm getting a little worried about him. I'll stay at home with him." She had Sabbath school with him and read him stories, but Georgie was listless. He didn't even join in the little Sabbath school songs that he loved so much. All Sabbath afternoon and all day Sunday he just lay around languidly, and his condition cast a gloom over everybody. Nafitalai hung around the back door, but Georgie didn't want to play. Miliana and Eseta waited around with woebegone little faces. "Isn't he better yet?" they asked Jessie and Agnes every few minutes.

"No, not yet," was all they could say.

Suddenly Eva appeared, and trying to force a smile, said, "Come on, children, let's play something. What shall we play?"

"We don't want to play," they whispered mournfully.

"Then what shall we do?"

"We'd like to pray for Georgie to get better," said Aganisi.

"Yes," agreed the others. And Nafitalai added, "Yes, why can't we children have a little prayer meeting all by ourselves?" So they poured out their little hearts in prayer several times during the day. But Georgie didn't get better.

Monday, September 19, came and Georgie was worse. The gloom now spread beyond the children and included the older ones in the village. Dear old Ratu Ambrose and Andi Kilera sat around and offered their services. But there was nothing that anyone could do. Georgie did not seem to be suffering much, but he was deathly quiet.

In the afternoon, all at once, he sat up and asked for a basin, and vomited up a quantity of brown blood. Then everyone knew that his condition was serious, very serious.

"Brother Ambrose, won't you join us in a season of prayer?" asked John. Ratu Ambrose couldn't reply, but one look at his tearful face told plainly that he was suffering as if little Georgie were his own son. So they all gathered around for prayer. Father

Fulton read the ninetieth psalm, about the Lord being our dwelling place in all generations, about the days of our years being three score and ten and full of sorrow, and including the prayer, "O satisfy us early with thy mercy; that we may rejoice and be glad all our days." Then he asked Ratu Ambrose to pray. Oh, what a prayer that was! The dear old man reminded God of the miracles He had wrought in changing *his* life from darkness to light, and begged God to work one more miracle and restore little Georgie to health and strength again. He paused as his tears made further speech impossible for a moment, then added the hardest words of all to say in prayer, "If it be Thy will."

Then Andi Kilera prayed, and Susie prayed, and John prayed. And God gave them all faith enough and trust enough to say, "If it be Thy will."

They waited and watched late into the night. Then John said, "Susie, I think you ought to try to sleep a little. Eva and Edith have promised to watch Georgie for a while."

"You ought to try to sleep too," said Susie.

"I will," answered John, and without undressing he lay down on the bed. Maybe an hour went by.

"I can't sleep," whispered Susie.

"I can't either," said John.

There was another pause, then, "John, do you remember the three temptations John Cole said God permitted to come to test all of His workers?"

"Yes."

"Appetite, ambition, and faith in God?"

"Yes, I remember."

"Well, we passed the first and second all right, and now this is the third."

"Yes, and it is the hardest one of all."

"John, I know that whatever happens, God loves us. But the temptation to doubt is so real."

The Fulton family in 1903.

The grave of John Fulton's son, Georgie. The inscription reads:
"George Lorin Fulton
April 4, 1897—Sept. 20, 1904
Until the day breaks."

"Yes, dear Susie—very real."

They were quiet for a little longer. John looked at his watch. It was midnight. Quietly he arose and walked out into the night—to his Gethsemane—and there he spent the rest of the night in prayer. He prayed and he prayed, "O my Father, if it be possible, let this cup pass from me: nevertheless not as I will, but as thou wilt." And as he prayed, his sweat fell in great drops to the ground. The temptation to doubt was indeed great, but he prayed till he could say, "O my Father, if this cup may not pass away from me, except I drink it, thy will be done."

In the morning John sent some of the boys to Suva again, to try once more to bring the doctor if possible. Then they took turns watching little Georgie, wiping his forehead from time to time, fanning him to make breathing a little easier, and hoping for some sign that he was past the crisis and would soon begin to mend.

At ten minutes past three o'clock that Tuesday afternoon, September 20, 1904, while Father Fulton was fanning him and Edith was watching, little Georgie looked up into his father's face. He opened his lips as if he were going to speak, and breathed his last.

"He's gone," whispered John. "O God, he's gone!"

Edith rose quickly and left the room. Eva was bringing in an armful of clothes from the clothesline. "He's gone," whispered Edith.

"He's gone."

"He's gone," they repeated from one to another till the sad news was known everywhere.

Brother Currow went to Suva and brought back a little coffin. In harmony with the customs at that time, Georgie was dressed in a white shroud, and the little coffin was placed in the church to await burial the next day. The grave was dug on the side of the hill between the mission house and the bay. All through the night loving friends took turns watching beside the little coffin in which lay the remains of a little boy who had meant so much to them all.

The next day little Georgie was laid to rest. John preached the sermon, Arthur Currow read the scriptures, and Ratu Ambrose prayed the prayer. It was a sad day.

"Oh, John, how I hoped that God would work a miracle and restore little Georgie to health and strength again," moaned Susie, as they lay sleepless on their bed that night.

"I had hoped too," said John.

There was a pause, then, "John."

"Yes?"

"John, could you get the letter—the one Sister White wrote to Uncle Samuel. Do you know where it is?"

"Indeed I do, Susie. It is right in my file. I have already read it several times. But I'll gladly read it to you again." John went to the file and was back in a moment. He read it all. In it he had underlined these sentences:

"In the weak state of your body, the enemy may try to make his voice heard that the Lord does not love you. O, he *does* love you. . . . I have *evidence* the *very best* that God loves you. . . . The cloud may appear dark to you at times in itself, but when filled with the bright light of Jesus, it is turned to the brightness of gold, for the glory of God is upon it."

"What precious, comforting words!" whispered Susie. "How I thank God for Sister White."

"I do too," said John. "Susie, though I cannot understand why God has permitted it, I am trying to say, 'The Lord gave, and the Lord hath taken away; blessed be the name of the Lord.'" His voice broke, and it was some time before he could add, "Susie, can't you try to say that too?"

But Susie couldn't speak. The words simply wouldn't come out. She could only take John's hand and squeeze it gently.

For a week or two Susie walked around as in a daze. Not infrequently the children would find her on her knees behind the blackboard in the church, praying. Not infrequently John heard her sobbing in her sleep and knew she was dreaming of her sorrow.

"Sometimes," Ratu Ambrose confided to John, "we find that caring for another little child helps a mother to get over her sorrow. I am told that in the village of Namarai on the Ra Coast there is a little baby girl two months old whose mother died when she was born. Her father, Solomoni, is doing the best he can to raise her, but maybe he would be glad to loan her to the Marama. And who can tell? Maybe it would help to lift the weight of grief that is weighing her down."

"You are very wise, Ratu," said John. "I'll plan to take the whole family on a little trip to the Ra Coast. And, as if by accident, I'll let Susie discover this little motherless child and we will see what happens."

So, just for a little change, and to get away from the house of sadness for a few days, the whole Fulton family got aboard the *Andi Suva* and sailed away up to the Ra Coast. They stopped in and visited with Ratu Meli at Nambukandra a day or two, treating the sick, and preaching the gospel as they were accustomed to do. Ratu Meli wept with them as he heard of their great sorrow at losing little Georgie, and tried to comfort them as best he could. Then they went on to Namarai not too far away to visit some of the believers. While they were there Solomoni brought his emaciated baby girl for Susie to treat. She had sores all over her. Her mouth was covered with thrush (small suppurating pimples). She was a pathetic sight.

"Where's her mother?" asked Susie kindly.

"She's dead," was the sad reply.

John, the children, and Eva were there looking on, stunned with the hopeless appearance of the little one. John watched

Susie intently. He wondered what she would do. He didn't have to wait long before finding out, for Susie looked at the baby, then its father, then at the baby again. Then she said, "John, this poor man can't look after this little baby. It needs more than one treatment. It will take many days to make it better. Don't you think I should take it home and look after it for him?"

John swallowed hard, then replied, "Just as you wish, Susie."

The father of the sick baby said, "Oh, thank you, Marama."

The children said, "Oh, yes, Father, let's take the little one home with us."

Susie reached out her hands and took the little one into her arms, sores and all.

"Let us call her Loloma," suggested the children, "for *Loloma* means 'love.' "

"All right," said Susie. "We will call her Loloma."

On the way to the launch they stopped at a little Indian store to buy some cloth to wrap around the little sick baby, and Susie's heart began to mend from that moment.

At Mburesala

IT TOOK A LITTLE TIME for the news of Georgie's
death to reach the Parkers at Loma Loma, but as soon as Calvin
heard of the Fultons' bereavement, he sailed over to do what he
could to comfort them. He was glad to see Susie quite occupied
with caring for little Loloma, and as soon as he thought it wise
he said, "Well, John, I suppose the next big job is the establishing of a training school."

"You're quite right," replied John. "And, Calvin, I have
£250 [$1,000] with which to buy land. Have you found a place
that might be suitable?"

"No," said Calvin, "but the last time I was in Levuka, one of
our church members there, Mr. Merrick, said he had heard that
John Morris who owns six hundred acres on the opposite side
of the island might be willing to sell part of his plantation."

"Good," replied John. "As you know, Calvin, Septimus Carr
is arriving on the next boat from Australia, and if we can't find
anything closer we will run over and take a look at it."

As Calvin was about to sail back to Loma Loma, he called
out, "Remember, John, I have three young men who are ready
to go to school and who are willing to help with the building as
soon as you say the word."

In the month of October, 1904, soon after graduation, Septimus Carr arrived in Fiji. The whole mission family from Suva Vou went down to the wharf to meet him. John shook his hand warmly, and said with a big smile, "Well, Brother *Ngginggi ni Vanua,* we are all ready for you."

At this everybody laughed except Edith, whose cheeks blushed slightly as she shook hands. Septimus knew that she was just as glad to see him as he was to see her. Sep, as they called him for short, was taken in the *Andi Suva* to the mission at Suva Vou, where he was given a warm Fijian welcome.

"Well, Sep," said John, "as soon as you have had a few days' rest, we will set out to search the land for a school site."

"*Vinaka! Vinaka!*" replied Sep, for he could already speak a few words of Fijian. And sure enough, in a few days off they went. "We will look at a few villages on the Rewa River first, then go on to the Ra Coast," said John. Their course lay within the reef to the delta of the great Rewa River. The scenery was magnificent, and Sep enjoyed every minute of it. They visited several villages, then one Sabbath day they found themselves just too far from an Adventist group to worship with them, so they anchored in midstream and were having Sabbath school all by themselves, when they saw an Englishman signaling them from the riverbank. They had a little rowboat that they always pulled behind the launch to enable them to go ashore when the water was too shallow for the launch, so they sent two of their boys to bring the Englishman to the launch.

"Good morning, gentlemen," he said as he stepped on board. "I am a doctor and would very much like you to take me to a village about ten miles upstream. Of course, I would be glad to pay you."

"Is there someone seriously sick up there?" asked John.

"Oh, no," said the doctor, "I just wanted to go up and look at some cattle that I hear are for sale."

"Then I am sorry, doctor," said John, "but we could not go up on business today. Of course, if it were a case of looking after sick people that would be different. But you see, we are Seventh-day Adventists, and today is God's rest day."

"What? You are Seventh-day Adventists?" asked the doctor in stunned surprise. Then he happened to look down at a paper on the seat beside him, and he saw the name *Present Truth.*

"*Present Truth!*—Adventists!" he gasped. "Whoever would believe that away out here in the jungles of Fiji I would find Adventists and a *Present Truth!* I used to see that paper often in England. You Adventists must be the greatest publishers in the world!"

Before their visit was over, the doctor discovered that the Adventists were indeed great publishers and great missionaries too. He left to find some other way to go to the village ten miles up the river.

The next day they went through the man-made canal that formed the northern branch of the Rewa delta. They went past the little island of Mbau, then about fifty miles north to Ratu Meli's village, where they had a good visit.

"Have you found a place for the training school yet?" inquired Ratu Meli eagerly.

"Not yet," replied John. "We were hoping you might have found something that you could suggest."

"No, I have not heard of any place being for sale," answered Ratu Meli.

"Calvin Parker has heard of a place on Ovalau, part of a six-hundred-acre plantation owned by John Morris, that might be available," said John.

"John Morris?" said Ratu Meli in surprise. "I know that place. It is *vinaka sara* ["very good"]. It is central enough. The soil is excellent. There are plenty of coconut trees, and two streams of water. But I doubt if he will sell."

"I was really hoping for something on the main island," said John. "But if we can't find anything here on the Ra Coast, we will go to Ovalau next month and see if God will find a place for us there."

"Why next month? Why not now?" asked Ratu Meli.

"Well, there are two reasons. I'm expecting Pastor E. H. Gates to go with me to help make the decision, and he is arriving in January. The other reason is that Brother Carr and our Edith are to be married on February 1, and we must be back home for that."

"*Vinaka, Vinaka!*" said Ratu Meli. "I am happy for them. *Vinaka, Vinaka.*"

Leaving Ratu Meli's village, they traveled north a few miles and came to the village of Namarai. "This is where we found Loloma, Sep," said John. "Let us stop and see if we can have a meeting with these good people."

"*Vinaka, Vinaka,*" said Sep, eager for every kind of new experience.

They anchored the launch, and leaving some of their young men in charge, followed the path up to the house of the village chief, Ratu Sekaia. After the usual polite introductions, John suggested that they had time to hold a meeting in the chief's house.

"No!" said Ratu Sekaia quite emphatically, "I do not want the Adventists to hold meetings in my house. I am a Wesleyan and that is enough. I used to be a heathen and lived in continual fear of the evil spirits."

"But I'm sure you do not fear the evil spirits now," interrupted John, seeing an opportunity to be agreeable.

"Not now. But our fear was very real in the old days. I remember well when I was young, a company of men from my village were coming back from Thakaundrove, the eastern province of Vanua Levu, where they had been working, and on the way they stopped on a little island for the night. On that island were many trees of a certain kind whose wood was considered sacred by the Thakaundrove people, for their god Ndakuwangga. They said that if anyone but the Thakaundrove people as much as touched it they would die. However, some of the men from my village laughed at the idea. 'It's just an old heathen superstition,' they said. So they freely gathered some of the sacred wood and used it for firewood. Of course, nothing happened—that night. But the next day while coming home, the angry god suddenly caused a strong wind to blow. Then big sharks came up out of the water and capsized the boat."

At this point Ratu Sekaia's eyes opened wide, and he lowered his voice to a whisper as he added, "And every man who had even touched the sacred wood was eaten up, but the others swam safely to land."

There was silence for a while, then John said, "The people of the *Lotu Savasava* do not fear the evil spirits, but we are also careful not to offend anyone for what he believes."

"Oh, yes, I've heard——" said Ratu Sekaia, then paused. John went on, "And there are many people in many villages who belong to the *Lotu Savasava* now, and we are going to establish a training school as soon as possible. My friend here, Misi Carr, will be the principal."

"Oh, you will?" said Ratu Sekaia. But it was quite plain that he did not wish any further conversation, so the missionaries politely took their leave.

Little did they know that Ratu Sekaia had an eleven-year-old son named Semi who, unknown to them, was listening to the conversation. But Semi had heard every word. His sharp eyes had taken in the clean upright appearance of the *Lotu Savasava* missionaries. He liked everything he saw and heard, and as the men walked back to the beach to board their launch again, young Semi scampered down the path behind them saying to himself, *"Lotu Savasava!* Training school! *Lotu Savasava!* Training school!"

"Well, you see, Sep," said John, "we don't always get what we want every time. But you wait. I'll come again, and the next time it may be different."

From Namarai they went farther up the coast to Nanukuloa, Ratu Joni's town. Here they were accorded a royal welcome and were given a further hearty approval of the Morris property on Ovalau—*if* Mr. Morris would sell. The more they heard about the Ovalau property the more they felt that the Lord was leading in that direction.

They returned to Suva. And soon things began to happen rapidly for everybody. Pastor and Mrs. E. H. Gates arrived for their visit, and on February 1, John Fulton had the pleasure of uniting Edith Guiliard and Septimus Carr in marriage. It was a happy day for everyone.

Two days after the wedding Pastor Gates, Sep Carr, and John Fulton, with three Fijian young men for a crew, went aboard the *Andi Suva,* and set out for Ovalau. First they called in at Levuka and visited with Brother Merrick. He gave them directions on how to find Mr. Morris at Viro, sixteen miles away on the other side of the island, and wished them good success. The next day they went to see Mr. Morris. They told him about their plan to establish a training school, and said that they had heard he might be willing to sell three hundred acres of his plantation.

Mr. Morris took them over to the little bay next to his. "We call this Mburesala," he said. "It has a good anchorage, a splendid beach, and three hundred acres of the finest land you could wish for. But I'm not too sure that I want to sell it. How much money do you have to put into it?"

"Two hundred and fifty pounds," said John.

"Only two hundred and fifty pounds for three hundred

acres?" he gasped. "Why that's ridiculous! No, no! I won't sell for that. I didn't especially want to sell anyway."

Pastor Gates and John tried again, stressing the fact that the training school would be training preachers and teachers to help dispel the darkness in old Fiji. But still Mr. Morris was not impressed.

"Then maybe you would lease the plantation to us, and let us pay rent on it year by year?"

"Lease it! Well, that sounds better. How long a lease would you want?"

"What about a ninety year lease?" suggested John.

"Ninety years! Why, no. I wouldn't be alive by then. I'd sooner sell and be done with it," declared Mr. Morris.

"And we would rather buy than lease," said John and Pastor Gates together.

"Well, what about three hundred pounds [$1,500 at that time]? That's only a pound an acre!" said Mr. Morris.

"I'm sorry," said John, "but all we have is two hundred and fifty pounds. This money has been given in small donations by thousands of Adventists all around the world. We couldn't hope to get any more than that for a long, long time."

"Two hundred and fifty pounds!" Mr. Morris was quiet as he thought for a moment. And as he thought, John and Pastor Gates prayed silently. After a moment Mr. Morris said, "All right. I'll give it to you for two hundred and fifty pounds."

And with all possible speed, the papers were drawn up and signed. The money was paid, and Mburesala belonged to the *Lotu Savasava.*

At once some Fijian workmen from Mbureta, a village about two miles away, were hired to put up four temporary Fijian houses, each twelve feet by eighteen feet. Then the *Andi Suva* hurried back to Suva, so the men could spread the glad news. On the way they stopped in and told Ratu Joni.

"Vinaka," he replied. "I'll get word to Beni and I'll have him ready by the time you return."

They stopped in at Ratu Meli's place and asked him to get word to Samuela and Jekope up in the Tholo district. *"Vinaka, Vinaka,"* he replied joyfully. "I'll try to have them ready."

As soon as they landed in Suva, they sent word to Calvin, telling him the good news and asking him to bring over Wesele, Kameli, and Timothi.

All was excitement at Suva Vou. Old Tevita's three sons Setereki, Jemesa, and Maika, were all going. So was young Nafitalai. You couldn't stop him. Edith was busy packing up, for she was going to Mburesala too. In fact, this was to be Sep and Edith's honeymoon.

At last the day came when, with John as the captain, the *Andi Suva* was to go back to Mburesala. Sep Carr and Edith and the four Suva Vou students got on board with their luggage, and amid waving of hands, happy cheers, and farewell tears, off they went. They picked up the two boys from the Tholo district at Ratu Meli's place, and Beni at Ratu Joni's place, and within a few hours more they were anchored in the little bay of Mburesala. They found two of the temporary houses ready to be occupied, so Sep and Edith moved into one of them and the boys moved into the other. In a few days Calvin and Pauliasi arrived with their three students in the *Ramona,* and by the time the third house was finished, in February, 1905, they opened school.

It was a humble beginning, with only ten students. But it was a veritable school for the sons of the prophets. They studied in the mornings and worked in the afternoons. They planted gardens and put up additional buildings. Within a few weeks four more students came—Mosese, Timothi Navara, Tevita, and Naimbuko. Smiling all over, John said, "Well, Calvin, another of our dreams has come true."

"Yes, indeed," agreed Calvin.

"You know, Calvin, I think we ought to move over here and make this our headquarters."

"You're right, John, and we ought to bring the press over and do the printing here."

"Right again!" said John. "We must move over here as soon as possible."

It was no sooner said than done, or at least begun. While their house at Suva Vou was being carefully taken apart, the Fultons moved in and camped with the Arthur Currows. Then in March the lumber and sections of the house were loaded into a banana barge and towed over to Mburesala by the *Andi Suva*.

Then the *Andi Suva* came back to take the Fultons and their hand luggage over. The bed bundles, trunks, and suit-cases were carefully loaded onto the launch, then the Fulton family went on board and sat on top of the luggage. Susie let Eva hold Loloma. Aganisi held her favorite pet—a mother cat —in her lap and did her best to keep it from getting panicky. Jessie held a cage on her lap. In it was her prized pet, a myna bird that she had rescued and nursed back to health and strength again.

Arriving at Mburesala, Eva, Jessie, and Agnes moved into one of the Fijian houses that the boys had put up for them, and John and Susie moved into another right next door to it, and there they lived while their lumber home was being reassembled. Next, the printing press was brought over and set up temporarily in another Fijian house.

Everything and everybody prospered in Mburesala during the next three months. When he was a boy in Oregon, John had often seen the early pioneers sawing their own lumber by hand with a pit saw, so now he taught the boys how to use a pit saw, and soon a new European house was erected for the Carrs.

Top: Fiji Mission Press building,
Suva Vou, Suva, Fiji.

Middle: Seventh-day Adventist
printing office, Mburesala, Fiji.

Bottom: First press used
by Seventh-day Adventists in Fiji.

181

Next a new Wharfdale Royal Cylinder press that could be turned by manpower arrived and was set up. Little Loloma's sores healed up and she became a very contented little member of the family. And Aganisi's mother cat had kittens, two of them!

In June the school was dismissed for a two-week midyear vacation. "Now, boys," said John, giving the students their parting instructions, "I know you are all enthusiastic about our new school. But as you can see we do not have room for any new students at this time. We will keep on building and maybe next year we will be able to take a few more. But remember! Not now! You must not bring back any new students this time." The instruction was clear. Everyone understood what it meant and why it was given. Nevertheless when Jekope returned, he was accompanied by a boy who lived in the mountains.

"And who is this?" inquired John with some misgivings.

"My cousin Mitieli," answered Jekope.

"And where is he going?"

"He wants to come to school, Misi Fulitoni."

"But don't you remember what I said?"

"Yes, Misi Fulitoni. I told him what you said, but he wanted to come so much."

"I know," said John sympathetically, "but where can he sleep?"

Groping for some small ray of hope, Jekope answered eagerly, "Oh, Misi Fulitoni, never mind, he is only a small boy. He can share my bed and my blanket."

"Yes, but how can we *feed* more students?" continued John.

"Oh, Misi Fulitoni," said Jekope earnestly, "never mind. I will take my serving of food each mealtime, and I will give Mitieli half of it, if only you will let him stay."

Who could withstand such pleading? John certainly could not. So Mitieli stayed.

All went well for a week or two, then one morning Aganisi couldn't find her two kittens. She went everywhere calling, "Kitty! Kitty!" but no little kittens came running to her call. The mother cat also followed her around calling "Meow, Meow," but no little kittens appeared from any place. Over to the printing office she went and in tears said, "Daddy, I can't find my kittens anywhere."

"Did you look in the garden?"

"Yes."

"Did you look in Eseta's house?"

"In Eseta's house? Why no. Do you think she might be playing with them?" And off went Aganisi.

"Eseta! Oh Eseta!" she called. "Have you seen my kittens this morning?"

"No, I haven't," said Eseta. Then her eyes opened wide as she added woefully, "Aganisi, haven't you heard what has happened to them?"

"No," said Aganisi, all ready for a fresh outburst of tears. "What has happened to them?"

"Well, you know that new small boy?"

"Yes."

"The one that came back with Jekope?"

"Yes."

"Well, they say that last night he caught your two kittens, and he skinned them, and he roasted them between two green bamboos, and this morning he ate them for his breakfast! So you'll never see your kittens anymore."

"Cannibal!" shouted Aganisi angrily as her tears rolled down her face. "Cannibal! That's what he is! I'll teach him to eat my kittens!" And taking no council from anyone she broke off a long switch from a nearby tree and waited behind the toolhouse for school to let out at noon.

At last the *lali* sounded. It was time for the students to eat.

One by one they came out of the schoolhouse and started down the path toward the school kitchen. Among them was small Mitieli.

"Mitieli!" called Aganisi. "Come here. I want to talk to you."

Hearing his name called, Mitieli came to the side of the toolhouse. They called him *small,* but it was only in comparison to the other full-grown boys. He was still a giant compared to eleven-year-old Aganisi. But filled with righteous indignation she said, "Mitieli, why did you eat my kittens?"

There was no reply. Aganisi went on with a scalding hot tongue lashing that included the keeping of the eighth commandment, and the difference between clean and unclean meats. Then she said, "Now I'm going to punish you. Turn around!" And he did, and Aganisi did punish him. She brought the switch down on his back again and again, till she thought he had had enough, then she let him go.

All of a sudden Aganisi realized that sooner or later a similar punishment would probably be meted out to her. She decided not to tell a soul. And Mitieli did not tell a soul, either. But somehow or other, the subdued atmosphere around both of them, with a little guessing here and there, gave Misi Fulitoni a pretty good idea of what had happened. John wondered for a time just what he should do. He had intended to say something to Mitieli and to punish him in some way, but finally he decided that Mitieli had had enough, so he dropped the matter. As for Aganisi he decided that she had probably had enough punishment in the loss of her kittens, and simply gave her a lecture on being kind and forbearing toward young men who came from villages where the people eat anything and everything.

Four months later it was time for the Week of Prayer in Mburesala. John was eager that Fiji's future workers would feel the need of praying together with the whole world family of Adventists, and would share in the great spiritual blessing that comes from it. So he carefully studied each article in the Week of Prayer readings, and presented it in Fijian to the school family each morning. When he came to the article by Elder W. A. Spicer, which gave a review of our worldwide work and appealed for a liberal offering to support this work, he hesitated a little. These dear boys have nothing, he thought to himself. How can I appeal to them for a liberal offering? But he did. He followed the plan and the reading as given to the world Adventist family. Then under the inspiration of the moment he said, "God never asks the impossible from us. You boys do not have money to give to His cause, but you do have hearts and bodies and strength. How many will gladly give their lives to the service of God?" Every student stood.

Next, although most of them had already been baptized or were in the baptismal class, he made a call for any who wanted to join the baptismal class to stand. Without a moment's hesitation, Mitieli stood. There were tears in his eyes and in the eyes of several others also.

The meeting was dismissed but the service was not finished yet. John went home and joined his family at the breakfast table. In a few moments they heard the sound of running feet and the shining face of Jekope appeared at the dining room door.

"This morning I gave my life to the service of God," he said almost breathlessly, "but I want to give some money too." He then handed John a one-shilling piece (25 cents at that time). "I had saved this money to buy a shirt with," he said. "But this morning when I heard about the great worldwide work, I thought of this shilling. And I want you to take it, sir, and send it to help the work go in the foreign fields." John's eyes filled with tears. His voice choked up. He could not speak.

But there was no need for words. Jekope had given *all* he had. God had accepted it as one of the greatest offerings of money ever given to His cause. And like the influence of the widow's mite, the influence of that one-shilling gift lived on for many years and influenced thousands of good people to put thousands of dollars into God's treasury.

His Heart Was
Always in Fiji

THAT WEEK OF PRAYER at Mburesala was the most satisfying inspiration imaginable to the missionary workers, but there was one cloud in the clear blue sky. Twelve-year-old Aganisi was sick. For a week or more she had complained of loss of appetite, headache, pain in her abdomen, and had had a little fever. Susie found that now her temperature was 103 degrees and kept her in bed. During the Week of Prayer they had special prayer for her, but she did not seem to get better.

After being in bed for about a week, a rash broke out on her abdomen, and then they knew that she had typhoid fever. Where she picked up the germs no one ever knew, but no typhoid patient ever had better nursing. Immediately orders were given for all of the drinking water for the school family to be boiled. And all other precautions were taken. The patient was limited to a little milk and oatmeal gruel, and her hair was cut off and her head shaved to make it easier to cope with the high fever. Aganisi longed for oranges. There were none growing at Mburesala, but that did not matter. One of the boys begged permission to go from village to village till he found some of the precious fruit. And who do you think that boy was?

Top: Boys' dormitory at Mburesala Training School, Fiji.
Bottom: Teachers and students at Mburesala Training School.

It was Mitieli—the boy who a few months before had eaten her kittens!

But in spite of all that was done, Aganisi continued to be very sick. One night she started up and called, "Mother! Where am I?"

"You are here in your own little bed, right beside me, dearie," Susie replied.

"Oh, I'm so glad," sighed Aganisi as she sank back onto her pillow. "I thought—I must have dreamed—that I was lying on the beach, and the waves were rolling up over me, and each wave was taking me a little farther and a little farther out into the ocean. Oh, Mother, don't let the waves take me. Don't let the waves take me, Mother!"

"I'll try hard not to let the waves take you, dearie," said Susie. And she tried her best to be cheerful and brave. But to John she confessed, "I'm so afraid she will be taken from us. We've lost one child. I just can't give up Aganisi too."

John was numb with sadness and fear, but he took his turn watching through the long dark nights, pleading with God and trying to hope. As Aganisi approached the crisis after three weeks of high fever, there seemed to be no hope left. The end could come at any moment. Tearfully John measured her, so that the boys could make the coffin when it was necessary.

But Aganisi didn't die! The crisis passed and she lived. Though she was left in a state of utter exhaustion for weeks afterward, the coffin was never made.

Aganisi was not the only one in the Fulton family who was having trouble. Eva had a stubborn tropical ulcer on her leg that seemed to defy every form of treatment. And John, for some reason or other, broke out in boils and carbuncles, crop after crop. "I don't like to tell the brethren in Australia how miserable I feel," he confided to Susie, "because I'm afraid they will make us go back to the homeland for a while."

"Well, I'm not afraid to tell the brethren that we need a change," said Susie. "Wasn't it Confucius who said, 'He who fights and runs away may live to fight another day'?"

"I don't know who said it, Susie," said John a little indignantly, "but I am not running away. And even if my body has to go for a change, my heart will still be here in dear old Fiji."

"Mine will too," replied Susie.

No doubt it was Calvin Parker who acquainted the good brethren in Australia with the pitiable condition of the health of the Fulton family, and soon a letter from Pastor O. A. Olsen, president of the Australasian Union Conference, arrived stating that the brethren recommended a change of work for John for a while. He asked John to be in Australia in time for the union conference session. The letter also called for Pauliasi Bunoa to attend the union conference as a delegate from Fiji.

The news was carried far and wide, from island to island, and from church to church. "Our Misi Fulitoni is going away!" they whispered to one another. "Our Misi Fulitoni is going to Australia, and we may never see him again."

The people came to say their fond farewells. From the mountains of the Tholo district came Ratu Beni. He presented John with a war club, a wooden fork, and a wooden plate, and said, "Misi Fulitoni, my father was a cannibal. With this club he killed many a man who was then roasted and eaten. As a small boy I also partook of the cannibal feasts. But the missionaries came and taught us a better way, a way of love. Then the *Lotu Savasava* came and taught us the clean way. We no longer use this war club, we no longer use this cannibal plate and fork, so I want you to take them with you. Show them to your people, and tell your people we thank them for sending their missionaries to teach us the clean way."

"I will," replied John as he counted the notches in the head of the war club, "and thank you very much. But, Ratu

Beni, it is only my body that is going away; my heart will remain in Fiji forever."

From the Ra Coast came Ratu Joni and Ratu Meli. Ratu Joni brought a beautifully carved canoe about four feet long, decorated with inlaid mother of pearl. "This is to remind you of the many journeys you have taken among us by canoe, and yacht, and launch," he said. Just then he caught sight of the war club and plate and fork. His eyes opened wide. "Misi Fulitoni," he said, "is this war club and wooden plate and fork not from Ratu Beni away up in the mountains?"

"It is indeed," said John.

"I knew it," said Ratu Joni. "For many years I have tried to buy that club from him. But he would never sell it. How much did you give him for it?"

"Nothing."

"Nothing?"

"That's right. You see Ratu Beni has been converted. He belongs to the *Lotu Savasava* now, and he wanted me to take them with me to show that he had turned from darkness to light."

"*Vinaka! Vinaka!* It's true! We all thank God for the *Lotu Savasava*. We will miss you so much."

"Ratu Joni, do not think for one moment that when I go away the work of the *Lotu Savasava* will stop. Other young men will come. Many more will come. Your own sons from the training school will become missionaries and preachers and teachers, and the Lord's work will grow and grow."

"But still we will miss you, Misi Fulitoni."

"Ratu Joni," John replied, "let me tell you what I told Ratu Beni. Only my body is going away. My heart will remain in Fiji always."

From Suva Vou they came—old Ratu Ambrose and Andi Kilera, and Tevita, still rejoicing in the third angel's message, and dear old Alipati. They saw poor Aganisi's short hair and emaciated condition. They saw John's boils, and they wept. "Oh, Misi Fulitoni," said Ratu Ambrose, "what would have happened to us if you had not come to Fiji? Do you remember how old Andi Kilera used to weep because of my wicked life? Do you remember that old pipe I had in my pocket? That was nine years ago when I threw that old pipe away, and God has kept me from tobacco and liquor ever since. Oh, Misi Fulitoni, the way of the *Lotu Savasava* is so good. I never want to go back to the old way again."

"Thank God for that," said John.

"We will miss you," said Ratu Ambrose. "We will have our yearly meetings, but you will not come. We will go to Mburesala, but you will not be there."

"But, Ratu Ambrose," said John, "let me tell you what I have told all of my Fijian brothers. It is only my body that is going away. My heart will always remain in Fiji."

Old Ratu Ambrose thought for a moment then said, "That's like what we said when you went to Mburesala. We said Misi Fulitoni has left us something that will remain with us till Jesus comes—the sleeping body of his little son, his only little son, Georgie. And every now and then we clean away the weeds from the path and from the grave. And then we say, 'Misi Fulitoni's heart is still with us. He can never forget us. And in the day of resurrection Misi Fulitoni will be with us again to get little Georgie.' Don't forget when the people in Australia learn to love you as we do and begin to call you 'Our Pastor Fulton' that you are not their Pastor Fulton. You belong to Fiji. You will always be Fiji's Misi Fulitoni."

The tears came to John's eyes. It was becoming harder than ever to say good-by. It was also becoming more and more certain that his heart could never leave Fiji. His heart would remain there forever.

Finally the day of their departure came. John's cloak of responsibility fell naturally enough on Calvin Parker. He accompanied them in the mission launch from Mburesala to Suva where they boarded the steamer for Sydney, Australia.

"So you're taking little Loloma with you, are you, Susie?" said Calvin.

"Oh, yes!" replied Susie. "She is one of our family now. She isn't two years old yet, and she needs a lot of care. Maybe when she is older we will let her come back."

As the *Andi Suva* pulled away from the beach at Mburesala the school family tried their best to sing "God Be With You Till We Meet Again," but it was no use. Their choked-up voices could not form either the words or the tune. Tears streamed down their faces. "We cannot let you go," cried one. The boys waded out into the water, as if to hold back the launch that was taking away their Misi Fulitoni. The whole Fulton family was also in tears. They had gone away before, but always there had been hopes of a speedy return. This time it was different. The thought that perhaps they would never come back to live in Fiji haunted them and broke their hearts. John looked at the boys standing in water up to their shoulders, waving good-by, and still weeping. He waved back to them and tried his best to say something. But all he could say was, "My heart—will always—be with you—in Fiji."

The Fultons arrived in Australia in February, 1906, and settled down to live in Wahroonga.

At the union conference session held about that time Pastor Fulton was appointed to be president of the New South Wales Conference, and dear old Pauliasi was ordained to the gospel ministry. What a happy day that was for John! Fourteen-year-old Jessie and twelve-year-old Agnes were enrolled in the little church school and quickly adapted themselves to life in Australia once more. Little Loloma grew round and fat as a butterball.

13

The next year, 1907, Jessie, then fifteen years old, went up to Avondale, and that same year a new missionary couple, Andrew G. Stewart and his wife, were appointed to Fiji.

"John," said Susie one day a few weeks before the Stewarts were to sail, "you know, I've been thinking lately that maybe I am not doing the right thing for little Loloma in bringing her up like a foreigner. Sooner or later she will be sure to resent being different from the other children here."

"And so——" said John feeling that Susie had much more to say.

"And so I wonder if we shouldn't send her back to Fiji with the Stewarts. She's well and strong and three years old now, and her own father, Solomoni, would have no difficulty rearing her now."

"Susie, you're right," said John softly. "I've often wondered if we were doing the right thing, but I wanted you to make the decision."

"Well, I have," said Susie. So when the Stewarts left for Fiji, little Loloma went with them.

The next year, 1908, Agnes, now fourteen, joined Jessie in the dormitory at Avondale. That was the year that Pastor Robert Hare came to Avondale as Bible teacher, and the Fulton girls met the Hare children, Reuben, Eric, Ruth, Nettie, and Enid.

In June of 1909 there was to be a General Conference meeting in Washington, D.C. John and Susie were invited to attend that meeting. As proof that John's heart was really in Fiji, he began the translation of *Early Writings* into Fijian while he was on the boat going to that General Conference.

When John returned to Australia he came back as the Australasian Union Conference president, and who do you think was on the same boat with him? John Cole and his family. He was returning to Australia as president of the South Australian Conference. I must leave it to your imagination to picture the joy and happiness that was theirs as they recounted their early experiences in dear old Fiji, and as John Fulton brought John Cole up to date with the latest developments—the ordination of Pauliasi, the arrival of the A. G. Stewarts and also of the G. E. Marriots, the transfer of the Sep Carrs and Beni Tavondi to open up a new mission in New Guinea, and the transfer of Calvin Parker and his family to Victoria, where he was to be president of the conference there.

"*Vinaka, Vinaka,*" sighed John Cole. "How I wish I had the health and strength to stay in Fiji myself. But I suppose we must let younger men carry the responsibility of the island work."

Soon after their return John Fulton decided to have Susie and his two girls live in Avondale so that the girls could have the advantage of a mother as well as a good school. He promised to spend as many weekends with them as he could, so for the next two years or so, during 1910 and 1911, Mrs. Fulton and the girls lived in Avondale village.

Now I have already told you that Robert Hare and his family had been living in Avondale village since 1908, so at last Susie and Henrietta were together again.

"Whoever would have thought in the old Healdsburg days that we would be in the same corner of the world, so near to each other, yet so far, that it would take twenty-three years for us to get together again!" sighed Susie.

"But they have been happy years, Susie, and just knowing that you were somewhere near has helped a lot," said Henrietta.

"And now just think, here I have a daughter as old as I was then!"

"Yes, Susie, you have two lovely daughters," added Henrietta, "and I have two sons and three daughters!"

"You have a wonderful family, Henrietta," said Susie, "and I hope we will all become better acquainted as the weeks go by."

And they did. At least two of them did, for one day soon

after that Susie dropped in to have a little visit with Henrietta, and she said, "Do you know, Henrietta, it looks like your sixteen-year-old Eric is a little bit interested in my sixteen-year-old Agnes!"

"Yes?" said Henrietta in perfectly simulated surprise.

"Yes. You know in the afternoons your Eric is chopping wood for the Health Food factory in the bush, about a mile past our place, and he finds it very convenient to stop in and fill his water bag at our place."

"Yes?"

"And my Agnes always drops whatever she is doing and goes with him to the faucet, then goes to the gate and waves good-by!"

"Well?"

"Well, Henrietta I just thought that maybe you would like to know."

"I had a pretty good idea that that was what he was up to," confided Henrietta. Then she added in a whisper, "Wouldn't it be wonderful if——"

"Oh, Henrietta, nothing would make me happier, but we musn't let on that we notice anything."

"Oh, no!" agreed Henrietta. "That might spoil the whole business."

So the two mothers, the two old friends of long-ago school days, watched a friendship grow between two of their children that later brought much satisfaction and happiness to them all.

By the end of 1911 John Fulton had decided that he needed Susie more than the girls did, so Jessie, nineteen years old, and Agnes, seventeen, were put into the girls' dormitory of Avondale College, while Father and Mother Fulton settled in Wahroonga.

At that same time Robert Hare went back into evangelistic work and was located in Adelaide, so their seventeen-year-old Eric was put into the boys' dormitory at Avondale. Well, by this

The mission launch *Dina* ("Truth"), Fiji, 1911.

Fijian girls.

time no doubt you have guessed that I was that Eric Hare, so after this I will use the first person pronoun.

By the end of 1912 Agnes had finished the business course and went to work in the sanitarium office in Wahroonga, where she could live at home. Jessie graduated from the teacher's course and went to Adelaide to teach in the Prospect church school.

By the end of 1913 I had graduated from the college course, and since I had developed a great burden to be a missionary to Fiji, the brethren recommended that I take the nurse's course in the Wahroonga Sanitarium. So, for the next two years during every spare moment I could find or invent, I was part of the Fulton family studying Fijian with Agnes.

Little did any of us realize what great changes were to come to all of our plans in the year 1915. This was the year when our great denominational leader A. G. Daniells was studying the reorganization of our world field. He visited Australia, then went on to India. The next thing we knew, a call came through for me to connect with the newly planned Karen Mission in Burma as dispensary worker, and Pastor Fulton was called to Washington to assist in the plans for the reorganization of the world field. He must have known there were great changes in the offing, for he sold all of his household goods, and advised Agnes and me to be married in June. With mixed emotions he performed our marriage service, then wished us Godspeed as we would proceed to Burma a few months later. Then bestowing the mantle of his office upon C. H. Watson, who was then vice-president of the Australasian Union Conference, John and Susie sailed off to the United States in July, with Jessie as part of their family.

With the mission fields developing so rapidly all around the world it had become necessary to divide the administrative responsibilities into several world divisions, and the Aus-

tralasian, Indian, and China unions were combined into the
Asiatic Division with headquarters at Shanghai. John Fulton was
made vice-president of this division, with R. C. Porter as president, and he went immediately to his new responsibilities. It
was not long, however, before failing health made it impossible
for R. C. Porter to carry on, so John Fulton became the president
of this new division. In 1916 Mrs. Fulton and Jessie joined
him in Shanghai, where Jessie was employed as a secretary in
the division office.

In 1917 Pastor Fulton's new responsibilities brought him
to India and Burma to attend the annual meetings of those
great fields. Jessie, of course, was still part of the family so she
was with them, and Agnes and I were fortunate to have them
visit us at our Karen Mission for a short time. It was lovely for
the family to be all together again, even if it was for only a few
weeks. We little knew, however, what great changes could
take place during just a few weeks, for it was during this visit
that Jessie met a promising young colporteur from Australia,
Harry A. Skinner, and to make a long story short, they were
married and pioneered the work among the Shans in Northern
Burma for the next twelve years.

Everything on our mission station seemed to remind John
Fulton of his early days in Fiji—the great Salween River,
the launch, the villages, the rice, the coconuts, the bananas. I
was just beginning to preach in the Karen language, but as yet
we had not broken through the heathen fear of their being eaten
by the foreign *dawtakas* ("cannibal evil spirits"). He encouraged us by telling again of old Ratu Ambrose, Pauliasi, and
Alipati. He told us of the tremendous influence Ratu Ambrose
and Alipati had had upon our people when they came to the
Australian Union Conference session in 1910. He told how he
and John Cole had started in Fiji with nothing, and that now
there were seventeen churches with 257 members. And his eyes

glistened with the joy of it. "Eric," he said, "I can never forget those days, and my heart is still there! My heart will always be in Fiji! It will be the same with you. The ones who will be born into the truth through your travail of soul will become part of your life, and you'll see, someday you'll know that no matter where you may go or what you may be doing your heart will always be here in Burma."

He paused for a moment, then went on. "There's to be a General Conference in San Francisco next year [1918], and I am to be there, and after that I am to attend the union conference session in Australia, and after that where do you think I am hoping to go for more council meetings?"

"To Fiji," I answered easily.

"How did you know?" he asked, looking surprised.

For a few moments I gazed intently into the eyes of this great man. He was my father-in-law, yes. He was the president of the Asiatic Division, yes. But he was more than that. He was a great missionary, Fiji's Fulitoni, and his heart was still in Fiji. As I gazed into those wonderful eyes, I knew that in my heart of hearts I wanted to be a great missionary too, just like him.

Agnes and I stayed twenty years on that Karen Mission station, and his words about our hearts always being in Burma all came true. And one of the things that helped us weather the sorrows and the hardships of those early years was the ever-present memory of this great man whose heart was always in Fiji.

The Great Awakening
in Central Fiji

FOR A FEW MOMENTS now let us note the movements of the indomitable Calvin Parker. Two years was all the rest as Victorian Conference president that he could think of. The brethren were looking for someone to open work in the New Hebrides Islands, and Calvin volunteered. They arrived at their new field August 11, 1912, and stayed there through hope and despair, through blood and tears, for four years. And they laid a foundation upon which younger men—Norman Wiles, A. G. Stewart, and J. Ross James—built a strong, vigorous church. By late 1916, the Parkers again needed a change of climate and surroundings. It didn't take him long to say, "Brethren, the work in Fiji is so well established, it is past the pioneering stage. Why don't we go back to Fiji? It will feel just like going home again."

The brethren considered their request, and finally agreed to send Calvin back to Fiji, this time to be president of the newly organized Central Polynesian Mission, which included Tonga and Samoa. Pastor Stewart, who had been principal of the Mburesala Training School from 1907 to 1916 and superintendent of the Fiji Mission from 1911 to 1916, was asked to take the Parkers' place in the New Hebrides. A new school family, the H. R. Martins, had arrived at Mburesala. Mrs. H. B. Meyers had been located in Suva since 1912, to head up the work for the Indians in Fiji. So Calvin Parker made his headquarters once more in Suva Vou, and entered wholeheartedly into his work.

The year 1917 was the third year of World War I. People everywhere were chafing at the shortages and the restrictions that the war had caused. Among those who suffered and were disappointed were the Wesleyan Christians in Central Fiji. Some of their missionaries had been recalled and inspirational visits had become few and far between. So it is not altogether surprising that a certain Fijian by the name of Sailose, away up in the mountains of the Tholo district, set himself up as a leader in dissension and began to draw a following after him. "Look," he said, "Britain is not as strong as she thought she was! See how long the war is lasting. Let us stop paying taxes. The British Government can't make us pay them. Anyway we are not keeping the right day. The *Lotu Savasava* is keeping the right Sabbath day. I would say let us all join the *Lotu Savasava*, only they are too strict. They won't let us use pork, lobsters, crabs, flying foxes, tobacco, or liquor. So come on, let us make our own free church."

This man Sailose created a lot of confusion and caused a lot of trouble. Of course, there were some who rallied around him. But the *Lotu Savasava* members called him a false prophet, and would have nothing to do with him. Sailose's followers naturally persecuted the Seventh-day Adventists wherever they could, and many of the Wesleyans accused the Adventists of being followers of Sailose. However for nineteen years Seventh-day Adventist tracts and the periodical *Rarama* had been distributed all over the country, and for twelve years our workers had been selling *Great Controversy*, so the people knew *about* the

Above: Touring through Colo, Fiji, in 1918. Calvin H. Parker in the foreground.

Below: Mission turn-out, Suva, Fiji.

Lotu Savasava. In the midst of this confusion hundreds of people hunted up the Seventh-day Adventist books and papers and began to study them.

"They are right," said some. "We are going to join the Adventists."

"We're afraid to join them," said others, "but we will keep two rest days, Saturday and Sunday, just to be sure."

At last someone suggested, "Why don't we ask the *Lotu Savasava* missionary to come up and explain what is the right thing to do!"

"That's right! That's right!" said many others. So at last they sent a delegation to Calvin Parker, begging him to come and visit them. Calvin hesitated, being reluctant to get mixed up with any political movement.

In six months another delegation came, larger than the first one. "Please come up and teach us," they begged. "Whole villages are keeping the seventh-day Sabbath."

Calvin counciled with the English provincial governor. After securing his approval, and the assurance that his movements would be completely understood, he called H. R. Martin from Mburesala and together they made the trip up into the Tholo district about August, 1918.

Up the Rewa River they went, then up the Wainimbuka River. They entered the town of Nanggia, where Ratu Josaia was chief. He was a terrible *yanggona* drinker. The use of this liquor had disfigured his face and dimmed and reddened his eyes. But he was not satisfied with his way of life. He welcomed our missionaries. The great *lali* was beaten and the village folk gathered for a meeting. Under the inspiration of the Holy Spirit, Calvin preached on the nearness of Christ's second coming, and asked those who wanted to be ready to stand. About one hundred rose to their feet. "We want to join the *Lotu Savasava*," they said. "And we want an Adventist teacher to live with us and to teach our children." Calvin wrote down their names.

Calvin looked at Brother Martin. "Do you think we could give them Sanipalati, who graduates this year?" he whispered.

"Maybe," whispered back Brother Martin, "but we had better not promise them definitely just yet."

Old Moape from the next village on the trail was there at that meeting. He had been an Adventist for several years, and his face glowed with joy at the interest he saw everywhere now. When the truth first found him, he was a user of every kind of unclean food and also of tobacco and *yanggona,* and his legs were so badly crippled that he had to use two walking sticks. But as he gave up his unclean foods and bad habits his crippled condition began to clear up, till at last he was able to throw away his sticks. "Are you coming to my town tomorrow?" he asked.

"Yes, all being well," Calvin replied. When he arrived old Moape, the cripple of a few years before, led the way and out-walked them on that fifteen-mile hike. They held another meeting in Moape's town, and got more names on the list. They were names of people already keeping the Sabbath, who wanted to study more and then join the *Lotu Savasava.*

Into the next town they went, and the next and the next. They found whole villages keeping the Sabbath. They were welcomed by the singing of choirs, and the number of names of those keeping the Sabbath grew and grew.

In some of the places they visited they ran into a situation where Sailose's followers and some of the Wesleyans were persecuting the Adventists, but Calvin's God-given wisdom, calmness, and integrity always won out and cleared away the misunderstanding.

Over the hills and down through the valleys they went, visiting town after town and village after village till they came at last to the village of Numbutautau, the village where Thomas

Baker was killed and eaten just fifty years before, in 1867. Calvin stood bareheaded before the little monument that had been erected on the spot where Mr. Baker fell. He thanked God for the wonderful change that the gospel had already brought to Fiji, and reconsecrated his life to the preaching of the third angel's message, which was to prepare some of these good people for the second coming of Christ. At the end of this thrilling visit to the Tholo district, Calvin had one thousand two hundred names of people keeping the Sabbath on his list! Do you wonder, then, that he was bubbling over with joy and enthusiasm when he attended the union conference session later that year?

John Fulton was also at that union conference session. At the General Conference session held in April of that year, the Asiatic Division had been divided. China was made a division by itself, and the Asiatic Division now comprised only Southern Asia and Australasia. John Fulton was still the president, so of course it was his business to be at this union conference session.

He ate up every word of the report that Calvin Parker gave of the progress of the work in Fiji, and spent every possible spare moment in Calvin's company asking countless questions about the school, the workers, and the recent visit to the Tholo district.

"How I would love to take a trip like that with you, Calvin," breathed John.

"I do wish you could," replied Calvin.

Now, of course, the committee brethren were glad to hear Calvin's glowing report, but maybe just to fulfill Habakkuk's prophecy, "I will work a work in your days, which ye will not believe, though it be told you" (Hab. 1:5), some of them smiled and thought Calvin might be exaggerating a little.

"I think we ought to send someone over with him to give him some help and carefully appraise the situation," said Elder Watson.

"So do I."

"So do I," agreed each of the committee members.

"How would I do?" suggested John Fulton, humbly. "I can speak the language. I know the———"

"Splendid! Splendid!" said Brother Watson. "All in favor say, Aye!"

The Ayes resounded from all sides of the room. So it was decided that John Fulton should spend some time with Calvin Parker appraising this movement in Central Fiji, and John was the happiest man in the world.

"Calvin, do you think that any of the one thousand two hundred people whose names you have written down have given up keeping the Sabbath by now?" asked John as they traveled on the steamer toward dear old Fiji.

"Perhaps *many* have, John, or will sooner or later," admitted Calvin, "but if we can get 10 per cent of them through the baptismal classes and into the church what a great victory that will be."

"It will be indeed!" agreed John.

"I don't like to change the subject," added Calvin sadly, "but you will miss dear old Ratu Ambrose. He died two years ago, you know."

"Yes, I heard that," answered John. "It's too bad. I surely will miss him. He was true and faithful, and a real shining light right to the end."

"Indeed he was. And Fiji is just not the same without the dear old chief and his smiling face," added Calvin.

"I will miss seeing Loloma too," said John sadly. "She died of dysentery in 1914 when she was just ten years old, while you were in the New Hebrides." Then John was quiet for a while, as he remembered a lonely little grave at Suva Vou, where a little boy was sleeping, *his* little boy, Georgie. He would miss him too.

As soon as possible after their arrival, Calvin and John set
out. They made the journey up the Rewa River by river
steamer. They had hardly started when a burly young Fijian
about twenty-five years of age approached with a big smile on
his face and said, "Are you not Misi Fulitoni?"

"Yes," replied John, "that is my name. You seem to know
me. Have you ever met me before?"

"Why, yes!" he said. "You preached a sermon in my village one day, when I was just a schoolboy about ten years old."

"That must have been fifteen years ago," replied John,
"and it's hard to remember schoolboys who grow up so fast,
you know."

"Yes, but I remember you," said the young man. "You
were selling little books called the *Great Controversy* for three
shillings each."

"Yes, I can remember selling many copies of *Great Controversy* for three shillings each."

"Well, I wanted one of those books so much, but all I had
was two shillings."

"And——"

"Well, you gave me the book and said I could pay you the
other shilling the next time I saw you."

"Yes, and——"

"Well, now, this is the next time I have seen you, and
here is the shilling."

From a fold in his belt he produced a shilling and handed
it to John. John was silent for a moment. Then he put that
shilling away very carefully and kept it for a souvenir for many,
many years. Into that young man's village they went and found
the truth spreading like wildfire.

Into the town of Nanggia they went. Ratu Josaia gave them
a royal welcome. Instead of a bleary-eyed *yanggona* sot, they
now found him well, bright-eyed, and alert, with the elastic

step of a young man, for he had reached out in faith and had touched the hem of the garment of Christ and had been made whole. Sanipalati was doing faithful work among the people. Every one of the one hundred whose names Calvin had written down, plus some additional ones, were still keeping the Sabbath, and Sanipalati had twenty-four ready for baptism. There were several old men in this town who had been cannibals. One remembered quite clearly when Mr. Baker had been killed and eaten up in the mountains. The old men all remembered how the *boom, boom, boom* of the great wooden *lali* used to call them to the cannibal feasts. But now they rejoiced when that *boom, boom, boom* called them to worship.

Calvin and John retired that night weary but full of joy, only to be awakened an hour or so later with the only too familiar hand clapping and dirgelike sounds that accompany a *yanggona* drinking party.

"Now what do you suppose all that noise means, Calvin?" asked John.

"Well, it isn't our Adventists, I'm sure of that," said Calvin.

"And I hope it isn't any of the people in the baptismal class."

"Or those that made their decision tonight," added Calvin.

The *yanggona* party noise continued an hour or more. Then, still greatly puzzled, the two men went back to sleep. In the early morning their puzzle was quickly solved. There was a knock on the door. Calvin opened it, and there stood four men. "Now we want you to write our names down," they said. "Last night we made our decision to belong to the *Lotu Savasava*. So we went right out and had our good-by *yanggona* party, and now we want our names written down."

"Good-by *yanggona* party!" said Calvin as he looked knowingly at John. "So that is what all the noise was about!"

"Yes, you heard it. Everybody heard it. Now everybody knows that we will never touch the stuff again."

14

And although both Calvin and John could have thought of a better way to say good-by to *yanggona,* they both felt greatly relieved and their hearts beat a little more freely after this candid explanation.

Before leaving Nanggia the whole village planned a feast in honor of the two visiting missionaries. Of course, there were some Catholics and some Wesleyans in the village, and as each family had a part in preparing the food, it was not surprising to see a roast pig and some *yanggona* root among the good things spread out on the banana leaves in the middle of the village common. The chief requested Calvin Parker to ask God's blessing on the feast. Seeing the things that God had cursed as food among the bounties, he hesitated a moment, then quietly requested them to first remove the pig and the *yanggona.* The Fijians saw what the difficulty was at once, and smilingly removed them. Whereupon Calvin asked God's blessing on the delicious abundance of fruits and vegetables and clean meats that remained. The people have long since forgotten what Calvin *said* that day, but no one in Nanggia will ever forget what he *did* that day.

Into old Ratu Moape's village they went. They found the old man well and happy, still walking around like a young man and rejoicing over the number that were keeping the Sabbath in his village. Calvin and John told him about the good time they had had in Nanggia and about the good-by-*yanggona* drinking party that followed their decision meeting. Old Moape smiled and said, "Yes, that is what many of us do when we become Christians. I did the same when I gave up *yanggona.*"

Into the next village they went, and into the next, bringing courage and good cheer wherever they went, and receiving satisfying spiritual meat for their own souls from what they saw God's Holy Spirit was doing.

They went into the town of Naimbita, and having arrived

early on Friday, planned to spend the Sabbath there. What a happy Sabbath day that November 23, 1918, was. One hundred and ninety-one persons by actual count were present for Sabbath school and the church service. A bright young man, also Moape by name, was in charge of the work there. He had twenty-one candidates ready for baptism. The attitude of all of our brethren there could be summed up in a speech made at the close of the afternoon service by their chief, Ratu Esala, one of the pillars of our church in this town.

He said, "Since we turned to the true religion, many chiefs and government officials have tried to intimidate us, saying we would be cast into prison on suspicion of being connected with Sailose's rebellious movement. But we are not followers of this false prophet. We are not opposed to the government. We are honest, loyal children of the light. If we are falsely accused and cast into prison, we shall go, knowing that God will care for us as He cared for Peter and Paul. We were not quick to accept the light of the *Lotu Savasava*. We took time to see what it did for others. But now we feel this is God's time for us, and we have accepted the truth, not because we have been forced to, not because we have hard feelings toward our former brethren, but because we need the cleansing power of the third angel's message to prepare us for the second coming of Christ."

Up, up into the mountains they went, and into the village of Numbutautau—the village where Thomas Baker was killed and eaten in 1867. They found the whole village of about one hundred people keeping the Sabbath. And Ratu Viliame Wawambalavu, grandson of the cannibal chief who committed the deed, was the leader of the group!

Ratu Viliame took John and Calvin to see the monument that marks the spot where Baker fell. He took them to the cliff over which his body was thrown into the little stream below. They climbed down to the foot of the cliff and followed the trail upstream, over which his body was dragged. They came to the great flat rock where his body was dismembered and prepared for cooking. They saw the remains of the old hot-stone oven where his body was roasted.

He took them to the nearby village of Mbialevu and introduced them to two old men who remembered well the death of Thomas Baker, and who actually partook of his flesh with their fathers at the cannibal feast. "Yes, we were young men then," they said sadly. "That was fifty years ago." Then a smile broke over their faces as they added, "But we are all Seventh-day Adventists now."

What a wonderful time they had during the few days they spent with these faithful brethren. John couldn't get over it. Again and again he said to Calvin, "I can hardly believe it. Only fifty years ago all cannibals, and now all Adventists!" On their way back to Suva Vou, John asked, "Calvin, how many of the twelve hundred people whose names you had written down did you find had gone back on their word and had given up keeping the Sabbath?"

Calvin replied, "Not even twelve of the twelve hundred. On the contrary, we have added hundreds more to the list."

"Well, I'll tell the brethren when I get back to Sydney," said John, "but I'm afraid they still won't believe it."

When John got to Sydney he said to the committee brethren, "It's all true. All that Calvin Parker reported is true and more! It is one of the most wonderful revivals that has taken place in the history of this cause." He then looked at Pastor Watson earnestly and said, "I know it is hard for you to believe. I think you yourself ought to go and see what God is doing in Central Fiji."

Brother Watson thought a moment then said, "I will." And he did. And he wrote the story of *his* visit in his book *Cannibals and Headhunters of the South Seas.*

Through the years John watched the church membership in Fiji grow as the members of the baptismal classes matured into full-grown Adventists. In 1917, just prior to the awakening in Central Fiji, they reported 17 churches with 257 members. In 1919 there were 32 churches with 671 members, and in 1923 there were 40 churches with 804 members!

Now in 1921, John Fulton was called to be president of the Pacific Union Conference in the United States. The next year, 1922, at the General Conference held in May, he was voted to be General Conference vice-president for North America. But before the year was out, Australia pleaded earnestly for John Fulton to be returned to them, because the same General Conference had called Pastor C. H. Watson to the General Conference Treasury Department. So the year 1923 found John Fulton again stationed in Australia as the president of that rapidly developing field.

He was as happy as he could be, and one day he said to Susie, "I have to go to the United States on sanitarium business this coming June and July, and what do you think I am going to do on the way?"

Susie smiled, for she knew the answer to that question. "You're going to Fiji. And I wish I could go with you."

"Yes, Susie. I'm going to spend a whole month in dear old Fiji. You see the Parkers had to go to Tasmania for a change of climate in 1921. We sent Pastor E. B. Rudge over to head up the work in Fiji for the next year, but now Fiji has the A. G. Stewarts back again as superintendent of the field, and I would just love to take a trip with Andrew Stewart up the Rewa River, and up the Wainimbuka to see what has happened to the wonderful work that is being done there."

John did visit Fiji. He landed there early in May. Again he was saddened to miss the familiar faces of dear old Pauliasi and Tevita, both of whom had passed away during the influenza epidemic of 1918 and 1919, but he was happy to see not only their children but also their grandchildren rejoicing in the truth. He was also greatly encouraged to see the group of new Fijian workers who were already in the field, and those who were still in training at Mburesala, where Pastor and Mrs. Sep Carr were again in charge.

Together John Fulton and Andrew Stewart traveled up the Rewa River. John recalled the story of the young man who five years before had recognized him on the river steamer and had paid him the shilling that he had owed on a copy of the *Great Controversy* that he had bought fifteen years before. They stopped and went into his village, Waisa, and there they found a thriving little church with a bright young preacher Asaseli in charge! Now Asaseli had been one of Andrew Stewart's pupils in Mburesala just a few years before, so he was more than delighted to see his old teacher, and in introducing him at the meeting that night he said, "I am so glad that my old teacher has come to see me that if I were a dog you would all see my tail wagging."

As John and Andrew traveled on to the next town, the whole village accompanied them for some distance before shaking hands good-by. Then as they moved on, the whole village broke into singing, "When the roll is called up yonder, I'll be there." John's and Andrew's heart beat faster, and they were strangely silent after the little hills and the trees shut off the sound of the singing.

They found newly organized churches in Nanggia, in Naimbita, and several other villages, and away up in Numbutautau there was another organized church, and Ratu Viliame Wawambalavu, the grandson of the cannibal chief who killed Thomas Baker, the Wesleyan missionary, was now the church elder!

A council meeting, more like a camp meeting, was held at Navua, a little town near the coast about thirty miles west of

Suva, at the close of John Fulton's visit. More than three hundred Adventists were present, including a number of new foreign missionaries, and Fijian preachers and teachers, together with church members and Sabbathkeepers still in the baptismal classes. Some had come two hundred miles in sailing boats across the ocean, some had come by canoe, while others had walked long distances to attend that meeting, and God was with them. It made John Fulton weep for joy as he saw the wonderful unity among the brethren and witnessed their reconsecration to God and the finishing of His work in Fiji. At this meeting plans were laid to establish a girls' training school at Navuso on the Wainimbuka River, and another school for Indian students at Samambula, not far from Suva.

"It was such a precious meeting," John wrote to Susie. "The Spirit of God was manifest as it worked on the hearts of the people." It was indeed a "precious" meeting. In fact, as John recalled, every meeting he could remember in old Fiji had been a precious meeting, and as he journeyed on to the United States and back to Australia the memory of these meetings brought immeasurable inspiration and power into his lifework.

Top: Fiji missionaries. Left to right: Mrs. George Marriot, John M. Cole, A. G. Stewart, Mrs. Stewart, a native helper, and George Marriot.

Bottom: A group of missionaries in attendance at the Fiji Mission council. Seated left to right: Calvin H. Parker, Ramona Parker, Sybil Reed, Mrs. Parker, Edith Carr, Mrs. Thorp, Elva Thorp. Standing: Septimus Carr, E. E. Thorp, John E. Fulton.

Fiji's Great Men

WHEN JOHN FULTON left Fiji in 1906 after almost ten years of service there, he told his beloved Fijian brethren that although he was going away the work of the *Lotu Savasava* would not stop. He told them that other young men—*many more*—would come, and that their own sons from the training school would become missionaries, preachers, and teachers, and that the Lord's work would grow and grow. But when he made that statement he had no idea how prophetic his words were, nor how literally they would be fulfilled.

Leafing casually through the *Yearbooks* from 1906 to 1966, I find the names of more than thirty families listed who have spent from two to thirty-two years walking in the footsteps of John Fulton. It is impossible to mention them all, but here are the names of a few of Fiji's great missionaries who served as long as John Fulton, or longer.

In 1903, Eva Edwards went to Fiji and in all gave twenty-five years in service, mostly in schoolwork.

In 1904 Sep Carr went to Fiji and altogether he gave twenty-three years of service connected with Mburesala Training School and in field work. Before they were married his good wife had already given nine years of service pioneering with

217

the Fultons, so Edith (Guiliard) Carr topped them all with thirty-two years of service for Fiji.

In 1907 the Andrew Stewarts went to Fiji. They gave fourteen years of service, three in the training school and he as president of the Fiji Mission for eleven years.

In 1908 Allen Butler joined the staff at Mburesala as teacher and bookkeeper, and served the field for nearly nine years.

In 1912 Mrs. E. Meyers went to Fiji and gave fourteen years of service to the Indian work there.

In 1915 the H. R. Martins went to Fiji and gave fourteen years of service to Mburesala.

In 1919 the Roy Lanes went to Fiji and gave seventeen years of service. Of these years, he spent two as secretary-treasurer, and three as president of the mission.

In 1920 the Cyril Palmers went to Fiji and gave ten years of service—eight to Mburesala, and for two he was president.

In 1920 the Gordon Bransters went to Fiji and altogether gave twenty-seven years of service to the work there. For one of those years he was president of Fiji Mission and for ten more years he was president of the Central Pacific Union Mission and was stationed at Tamavua.

In 1921 the Gilbert McClarens went to Fiji and gave eleven years of service.

In 1922 the E. B. Rudges went to Fiji and he gave eleven years of service as president of the mission.

In 1923 the George Masters went to Fiji and gave seventeen years to the Indian work there.

In 1925 the H. R. Steeds went to Fiji and gave eleven years of service.

In 1931 the L. V. Wilkinsons went to Fiji and gave thirteen years of service—eight to schoolwork and four years he served as president.

In 1932 the W. G. Ferrises went to Fiji and gave twenty

years of service; the last six years he was president of the East
Fiji Mission.

In 1933, the A. P. Dyasons went to Fiji, and gave twenty-
two years of service to schoolwork—seven years to Mburesala,
and fifteen years to Fulton College.

In 1946 the N. W. Palmers went to Fiji and spent ten years
there.

In 1948 the K. D. L. Brooks went to Fiji and gave ten years
to the Indian work.

The same year the C. S. Adamses went to Fiji and also gave
ten years of service. Part of this time was spent at Fulton College; the remainder he was president of West Fiji.

In 1957 the B. L. Crabtrees went to Fiji. Part of their time
he has been president of East Fiji and also president of West
Fiji, and they are still there.

In 1958 the R. K. Wilkinsons—second generation missionaries—went back to Fiji. They have already given ten years
to schoolwork and are also still going strong.

Hats off to these great missionaries and to all of the others
whose names have not been mentioned. But the half has not
yet been told.

It is a little more difficult even to estimate the number of
missionaries, preachers, and teachers that have been trained in
our Fijian schools and have gone forth holding high the torch
of truth, for the *Yearbooks* give only the names of the ordained
ministers and then the number of the other Fijian workers. But
it would be quite safe to say that more than one hundred faithful, consecrated workers have come from our training schools in
Fiji. I can only briefly mention a few, a very few, of Fiji's own
great men.

First let me mention Beni Tavondi. He was one of the
foundation builders at Mburesala. In 1908 when the brethren
called Sep Carr from Mburesala to open up work in Papua,

Beni and his good wife, Aliti, were appointed as their assistants. After a great deal of difficulty they purchased one hundred and thirty acres of land at Bisiatabu, twenty-seven miles from Port Moresby, and hired a number of Papuan workmen to clear the land. Beni quickly learned to speak their language and conducted morning and evening worship with them, but there was no response. He tried for four years, but there was no response. He wrote to John Fulton, who was at that time president of the Australasian Union Conference, begging for another Fijian helper so that they could try preaching in the villages farther inland. John Fulton in turn wrote to H. R. Martin at Mburesala asking if any one of the young men graduates would volunteer for work in Papua.

"Yes, we have a volunteer," Brother Martin replied. "It is Mitieli Nakasami."

Mitieli! What memories that name stirred up in the minds of the Fulton family, when John announced one day in 1913 that Mitieli and his wife, Fika, would be arriving in Sydney in a few days en route to Papua.

"Father, shall I say anything to him about my two kittens?" asked Agnes, who was now a young woman nineteen years old, working in the office of the Sydney Sanitarium.

"No, no, my dear!" said John. "I think you said enough about them long, long ago."

"Then I'm just going to be real nice," said Agnes, "and I'll show them around the sanitarium, and I won't say one word about the kittens."

Mitieli and Fika arrived. John was at the wharf to meet them. He brought them to the Fulton home for the three or four days they had to wait for their boat going to Papua. Agnes *was* real nice. She shook hands, and showed them all around the sanitarium. She talked to them in Fijian, about all of their old friends, but never once mentioned kittens. Nevertheless,

Beni Tavondi

John firmly declared, when Mitieli looked at Agnes and Agnes looked at Mitieli, he could very easily tell that they were both *thinking* kittens.

Well, Mitieli joined Beni and Sep Carr at Bisiatabu, and a close bond of friendship grew up between the two Fijian workers. In 1915 the Sep Carrs were invalided home to Australia and the Arthur Lawsons took their place. By this time Mitieli was able to preach and the two Fijians took turns reaching out farther and farther to the inland villages. On one occasion Mitieli set off alone, naming the village where he proposed to spend the weekend preaching. "I'll be back Monday morning, Beni," he said as he left.

Monday morning came, but Mitieli did not come. "He must be in trouble," said Beni. "I must go and find him." He found him in an empty hut, sick and alone, utterly forsaken by the heathen villagers he had gone to help. He had a raging fever. He ached all over.

"I knew you would come, Beni," he whispered. "I have taken some medicine but I don't get any better."

"I must get you back to the mission," said Beni. "Wait a moment. I'll try to hire some carriers." Beni tried, but there wasn't a man in the whole village who would help carry that poor sick preacher back to the mission station. "Never mind, I'll carry you back myself," Beni whispered into Mitieli's ear. And he did. Sometimes he carried him on his back, sometimes on his shoulders. He was often exhausted, he often stumbled, and often had to rest. It took him two days! But he got Mitieli back to the mission station in time to save his life.

They worked together for five years, but still there was no response—not one convert! Then one day in 1918 Beni was bitten by a venomous snake. He ran into the house and got the snake-bite medicine out of the medicine box, but in spite of all that he and Mitieli and their wives could do, Beni felt the poison coming nearer and nearer to his heart and he knew that soon he would die.

"Mitieli," he whispered, "I am going to die soon from the effects of the snake bite. Please call the workmen to my bedside. I want to talk to them and appeal once more to them to accept Christ before I go."

Mitieli called in the workmen. Silently and sorrowfully they stood by Beni's deathbed. Then, looking around at them, Beni spoke: "For ten years I have preached to you about Jesus, who longs to be your Saviour. For ten years you have heard, but made no response. I will soon die, and you will hear my voice no more. But before I go, I want to ask once more, Is there not *one* of you that is willing to forsake his heathen customs, and believe on the Lord Jesus Christ, and accept Him as his Saviour?" He could speak no more.

The workmen stood by, dumb with sadness, for even the heathen feel sorrow. Soon one began to sob, then another, and in the weeping that followed, one of the workmen said in a broken voice, "Beni, I will. I want to be a Christian." And as he spoke, another added, "So will I, Beni." And these were the first two converts in the Papuan Mission after ten long years. A look of relieved satisfaction came into Beni's face, and there was just a trace of a smile as he breathed his last.

About three years after Beni's death Captain G. F. Jones and his wife were asked to relieve the Arthur Lawsons while they took a much-needed six-month furlough. Captain Jones was a little man physically, but measured by faith he was a giant. He studied the situation in Papua, and little by little developed a burden for the villages of the great interior. One day he opened his Bible and his eyes rested on the verse, "Arise, that we may go up against them: for we have seen the land, and, behold, it is very good: and are ye still? be not slothful to go, and to enter to possess the land" (Judges 18:9). As he read, his heart beat faster. "This is God's voice calling me up into the mountains," he said to himself. Then he called, "Mitieli!"

Mitieli was there in a moment. Captain Jones read him the text. Then he said, "I think God is calling us to go up into the mountain villages *now.*"

"I think so too," said Mitieli.

"The verse says, 'Be not slothful.' That means go now."

"I'm ready," said Mitieli.

"Tomorrow is the Sabbath. Let us go and see what God will do for us," said Captain Jones.

"We will go," said Mitieli. And they did go. Up, up, up the mountains they went. They passed through one or two villages with no opportunity to preach, then came to a village where all was excitement. On the ground in the center of the village, writhing in pain, lay the son of the village chief. All around him the men of the village were leaping about, shouting and brandishing their spears. Captain Jones and Mitieli realized at once that this was the heathen ritual dance whereby they discovered the one who had brought the sickness or the curse upon the chief's son. They also realized that the turn of a hand could condemn them both to death at any moment. But Captain Jones did not hesitate. "Mitieli," he said, "get some hot water quickly. Then come and join me in prayer." Then lifting his hand to heaven, Captain Jones shouted, "Listen to me all you village men. I am the servant of the living God in heaven. The living God can make this boy better. Put down your spears, and be quiet while I talk to my great God." Out of sheer shocked surprise the chief and his men sullenly obeyed. Captain Jones talked on about his great God for a few moments, while Mitieli was getting the hot water. As he talked, the sufferer calmed down enough to take a drink of the hot water when it came.

Then Captain Jones prayed. He talked to God as one who knew Him face to face. And as he prayed, the suffering lad was

Mitiele and his family.

relieved. After the prayer, he walked over to his father and embraced him. It was a miracle! It was the work of the living God, and the old chief knew it. "Now," said Captain Jones, "you need a school and a teacher so that you and your children can be taught about my great God."

The grateful chief was ready for anything. And that was the beginning of the great breakthrough that resulted in mission stations, schools, and dispensaries being built all through the interior of Papua. Mitieli was one of the chief workers in this spectacular movement. He served in Papua eleven years and truly he deserves a place among Fiji's great men. He was always courageous, resourceful, patient, and Christlike.

His wife, Fika, was also a very remarkable woman, a veritable Deborah. She championed the cause of Papua's downtrodden women and girls, and defied the savage men of the jungles. At times she fearlessly snatched spears and war clubs from their hands. It is no wonder then that the people called her the woman warrior of Jesus.

But the story does not end here. Mitieli and Fika had a son, and to keep alive their rare friendship with Beni, they named him Beni Tavondi! Today that boy has grown to manhood and is one of Fiji's foremost evangelists. He has become skilled in the use of electrical equipment, and with a generator, loudspeaker, and projectors, he is figuratively turning Fiji upside down.

And even this is not the end of the story. Beni's widow, Aliti, returned to Fiji and in time was married to another strong young worker, Semiti Ngande, and can you guess where they went to work for the Lord? Yes, they went to Papua. Hats off to another of Fiji's great women and another great man.

In 1924 it was decided to open mission work at Efoge, fifty miles inland on the trail that had been blazed by Captain Jones and Mitieli. Nurse Emily Heise was to open a dispensary there.

Above: Ratu Semi and his wife.

Below: A group of Fijian pastors. Left to right: Nemani, Soleveni, Laitia, Epeli, and Jemesa.

She called for a Fijian assistant, and who do you think answered the call this time? Little Georgie Fulton's bosom friend now grown to manhood, Nafitalai Navara! Nafitalai, the little boy who played funerals and church services with Jessie and Agnes and Georgie!

Up into the great interior of Papua went Nafitalai with his brave wife, Vasiti. They served there for seven years, and then were granted a furlough back to Fiji, their homeland. When they returned to Papua in August, 1931, they were asked to pioneer the work on the islands of Emirau and Mussau in the St. Matthias group about 250 miles north of Rabaul, which is the chief city of the island of New Britain. So to the largest island, Mussau, went Nafitalai, Vasiti, and their two children—Tina, twelve years old, and Joe, eight. But the going was hard. The people were degraded and diseased by their filthy heathen practices, and showed no interest whatsoever in making any change for the better.

Into village after village with his Picture Roll went Nafitalai. Day after day, week after week, he sang, told Bible stories, and appealed, but every one of the two thousand inhabitants of that island seemed determined to keep on living in his dirty, filthy, heathen way. Then an epidemic struck the island and many people became sick. One of the first to die was an old man who had at least been friendly to Nafitalai, and strange as it may sound, his relatives requested Nafitalai to give him a Christian funeral. He did. But their expressionless attitude gave no hint that they were pleased. Then both Nafitalai and Vasiti came down with the fever. This, added to the indifference of the people, drove them to the verge of giving up.

In a day or two, however, a man came from a village ten miles away, with a request for another Christian burial, for his uncle. "I'm sorry," moaned Nafitalai, "but I'm too sick to move. I cannot go."

"But you must come," urged the man. "My uncle said the mission way was good."

"I'm sorry, but——" began Nafitalai. At this point, however, he was interrupted by Tina. "Father," she said, "why couldn't I go? I know the chapter in Corinthians that you read."

"But, Tina, my dear," said her father, "you're only a little girl. It would not be safe. These people are savages and might harm you."

"But, Father, Joe would come with me to protect me," argued Tina, and turning toward her little brother, she said, "wouldn't you, Joe?"

Eight-year-old Joe nodded his eager approval of the idea, and at last Nafitalai and Vasiti gave their consent. The two little heroes took their Fijian Bible and hymnbook and followed the heathen stranger to the village ten miles away. Tina directed them how to dig the grave, and how to wrap the dead man in mats. Then while two hundred heathen looked on, the two children sang, "Jesus loves me! this I know." Tina then read some verses from the fifteenth chapter of first Corinthians, and Joe prayed that angels would mark the grave of this poor man, and would resurrect him when Jesus comes. Then they walked ten miles home again—alone.

Within a few days two more requests came for Christian burials, and Tina and Joe went again and conducted Christian services for people who had given no outward indication that they were dissatisfied with their hopeless, squalid lives. Tina and Joe didn't realize it at the time, but this was the beginning of the breakthrough for Mussau. When Nafitalai was well enough to go preaching in the villages again, the people flocked to hear him and greeted him on every hand with smiles.

In due course other missionaries from the Solomon Islands came, and little by little the people began to come to Sabbath school. They cleaned up their clothes and their bodies. They built new villages. They forsook their old heathen customs, and today every person on the islands of Emirau and Mussau attends Sabbath school.

These are not all of Fiji's great missionaries who have gone to other lands to preach the gospel. It is difficult to find the records of all of them. You may, however, remember my mentioning old Tevita and his sons. Well, one of his sons, Maika Dauniika, and his good wife, Tokasa, also served in New Guinea, but only eternity will reveal the trials that they endured and the victories that they won.

Before this chapter closes I must mention another group of Fiji's great men, Fijian men who were delegates to some of our General Conference sessions in the United States. Fijian men who have become widely known and greatly loved throughout America.

Foremost of these is none other than Ratu Meli Salambongi. In 1926, while John Fulton was still president of the Australasian Union Conference, it was decided that he bring Ratu Meli with him as a delegate from Fiji to the General Conference to be held in Milwaukee, May 27 to June 14. It was also my great privilege to be a delegate from Burma at that meeting, and I had the pleasure of getting well acquainted with Ratu Meli there. What a man he was! He wore the Fijian *sulu* and walked barefooted, but he mingled with ease among the city's great men who came to do him honor. And when he talked in the conference meetings through John Fulton as his interpreter, he moved the hearts of the Adventist people mightily.

I heard him tell how his father accepted Christianity and became a Wesleyan preacher, and how he called Meli to his bedside when he was dying, and said, "My son, my end is near. We have been blessed in receiving light from the Word of God. It has been good, but it is not *all* the light. You will live to see another church come to Fiji which will observe the seventh day of the week as the Sabbath. It has not come in my time, but it will come in yours." Then Ratu Meli told how that church did come in his day, in the person of John Fulton. He told how reluctant he was because of his government position to step out and keep the Sabbath. Then in one of his apt Fijian figures of speech he said, "But once you have been convinced of the Sabbath truth you can't get away from it. It is just like a Fijian walking on coal tar with his bare feet, it holds! So I just *had* to take my stand."

He spoke humorously of his amazement at the wonderful things he saw in America—its houses, its gardens, its cities. "Why," he said, "everything over here goes with electricity. I hear voices on the radio. I see pictures in the newspapers sent across the ocean by radio. I can't get these things through my head, but they tell me it is some kind of electricity. In one of our schools I saw the young people washing dishes with electricity. Last Sabbath they took me around Chicago to preach in four churches. We went from church to church by motorcar. It also went by electricity. There was no time to stop for lunch so we had to eat in the motorcar, and it went so fast that I took a bite out of my sandwich in one part of the city, and swallowed it in another."

Then he won everybody's heart by saying, "When I was in Australia I saw a big mother hen trying to look after a large brood of chickens. It was hard for her to keep them all under her wings at the same time. This General Conference is like that big mother hen, and our islands in the ocean are like those many chickens. But I see in the map that the same Pacific Ocean that washes your shores also washes our shores. So I know we will be safe under your wings."

When the reports of the nominating committee were brought in, and Ratu Meli heard that John Fulton had been called to be the president of the Pacific Union Conference, he

Ratu Setareki Cevaca   Ratu Jaili

John E. Fulton, Ratu Meli, and Eric B. Hare.

got up and said, "In Fiji my neighbor doesn't mind if my horse eats grass in his field. But that doesn't make it *his* horse. It is still my horse. So we don't mind our Misi Fulitoni eating grass in your field for a while. But remember, that will not make him *your* horse. He will still be *our* horse. He will still be Fiji's Fulitoni."

Toward the end of the meeting in giving his testimony, he said, "I came to America on a great steamship. Before it left Fiji they pulled the United States flag to the top of the mast. Then the captain went onto the bridge. Soon the last whistle blew and the steamer started off. So, brethren, we are on the great Adventist ship soon to be going to the New Jerusalem. The flag, which is the Sabbath day, is up at the top of the mast. The Captain is on the bridge. Soon the last whistle will blow and the ship will start. It is time for us to get on board now. And I assure you that we from Fiji will be on that ship with you!" Everyone who saw and heard this great man, Ratu Meli, during that General Conference will remember him and the inspiration he imparted as long as he lives.

At the 1930 General Conference held in San Francisco, Andrew Stewart brought two more delegates from Fiji. Ratu Jaili (Charlie) Tui Lakemba, and Ratu Setareke Thevatha. The reports of their visit are meager, but John Fulton was also there. He was justly proud of these two sons of Fiji. He had known Ratu Setareke from the time he was a boy, when he lived in Suva Vou, and it gave him great pleasure to hear him telling of the progress of the work with such a pleasing, beautifully modulated yet powerful voice.

Ratu Jaili was also a soft-spoken, dignified, kindly gentleman, and he won everyone's heart when during one of his talks he said, "In America I have enjoyed very much listening to the music played on your pianos and on your organs. And I could not help noticing that these instruments have both white keys

and black keys. I asked someone why they had to have two
kinds of keys, and they said that if there were only white keys,
the music would not be so beautiful, and if there were only
black keys, the music would not be so beautiful. They needed
both the white keys and the black keys to make the music really
beautiful and harmonious. Then I knew why God needed both
American workers and Fijian workers to make the preaching
of the third angel's message beautiful and harmonious."

In 1950 Elder N. C. Wilson brought Ratu Semi Vuloaloa
as Fiji's delegate to the General Conference in San Francisco.
You may remember in Chapter XIII reading the story of a visit
that John Fulton and Sep Carr made to the village of Namarai,
when Semi was just a lad eleven years old, and how he overheard
the conversation about the building of a training school. Well,
in one of his talks at this General Conference, Semi told the
sequel to that story. "After that visit," he said, "I kept thinking
about the Mburesala Training School. I could not get it out of
my mind. My father, Ratu Sekaia, also kept thinking of the
Lotu Savasava. He couldn't get that out of his mind. So when
Misi Fulitoni came again to Namarai village, my father at once
requested him to hold some meetings in his house. After the
very first meeting my father had a dream. He saw a man clothed
in white garments who said to him, 'This is the true church.
You must accept it.' In the morning he couldn't get the
dream out of his mind. He thought about it all day long, and at
the meeting that night my father made his decision to be a
Seventh-day Adventist. Then he called my mother, my older
brother, Mosese, and me, and begged us to take our stand for the
Lotu Savasava with him. We did. When I was fourteen I attended
the mission school in our village. The next year I went to
Mburesala. After graduating from there, I went to Avondale,
and was there for two school years. And ever since that time I
have been a worker connected with the press or with the school."

It was a rare privilege for both Agnes and me to be able to attend that General Conference session also, and we were delighted to meet this good man.

It is impossible fully to record all the deeds of Fiji's great men, but these few examples are sufficient, I think, to show that true greatness begets greatness, and Fiji will always have its great missionaries and its great men walking in the footsteps of their great pioneer, John Fulton.

John Fulton's Reward

IN 1926, as has already been stated, John Fulton was called from the Australasian Union Conference to be president of the Pacific Union Conference. For the next six years he filled that post with honor. He proved to be an experienced administrator, a beloved counselor, a dependable burden bearer, and a tower of spiritual strength. By this time, however, he was sixty-three years of age and his interminable zeal and earnestness had begun to sap the life beat of his valiant heart, and he requested that the brethren give him lighter responsibilities. So in 1933 he was invited to be the president of the Northern California Conference.

For three more years he served that field to the great joy and happiness of its members. Then in 1936 he was called to be president of the Southern California Conference. He had all the ability that a president of so large a conference needed, but not the physical strength. His poor old tired heart could not bear up to the strain that such responsibility placed upon it, and at the end of the year 1936, at the age of sixty-seven, he begged the brethren to permit him to retire, and with great reluctance his request was granted.

When the brethren in Australia heard that John Fulton was

free, Pastor C. H. Watson immediately set the wheels in motion to bring him to Australia for one more visit.

"We want him too!" said Fiji. "We want him to attend our *bose*, July 14 to 18, 1937. Do you think that he can come?"

The invitation gladdened John's heart more than anything else could possibly have done. Of course he could come! John and Susie landed in Suva on July 6. Before long they were guests of Ruth and Roy Lane, in the same old house where they used to live long ago, for Roy Lane was president of the Fiji Mission at that time. The A. G. Stewarts and Pastor E. E. Roenfelt had come from Australia to attend that meeting also, so for a few days Ruth Lane had her hands and her house more than full.

As soon as John and Susie could steal away, they followed the little path to the cemetery not far from their old home, and stood arm in arm with their heads bowed by the grave of their little son. Silently they wept as the memories of those early days flooded over their souls and reminded them keenly of part of the price they had paid for the success of God's work in Fiji.

In a day or two the men set off and spent a happy week visiting some of the mission stations and schools that had sprung up since John had first started work there forty years before. They visited the graves of Ratu Ambrose, Ratu Pauliasi, in Suva Vou, and Ratu Alipati in Mburesala. "How well I remember them," said John. "They gave the cause of God all they had. I remember so well the first church we organized. How many churches do we have now, Brother Lane?"

"Fifty-three!" replied Roy.

"And how many church members?"

"Nine hundred and ten. And many more in the baptismal classes."

"I remember the first little church school we started in Suva Vou. How many do we have now?"

"We have thirteen church schools with five hundred and twenty of the brightest, happiest boys and girls you have ever seen."

"And training schools?"

"Mburesala, that's the training school that you started, now has about fifty young men. Up on the Wainimbuka River at Navuso we have another with about fifty young women in training. Then we have an intermediate school at Samambula near Suva with about one hundred Indian students, and another over on the large island of Vanua Levu at Vatuvonu with eighty students."

"I can hardly believe it," breathed John, "but keep on, Brother Lane. How many ordained Fijian ministers do we have now?"

"Ten. There's Methusela, Mitieli, Timothi, Sanipalati, Jope, Josaia, Semi, Semite, Maika, and Setereki."

"Yes, I know them all," said John. "I remember when we had only one—Pauliasi. And how many other Fijian workers, teachers, press workers, and colporteurs do we have?"

"More than forty!"

"Wonderful! It's so wonderful that it's hard to believe," exclaimed John.

At last the day came for the *bose* to begin. The tiny island of Nukulau about twelve miles from Suva was put at their disposal. Nukulau was a beautiful little island about one mile in circumference, just like a park. It had a big roomy house, and an abundance of coconut palms. Temporary shelters had been erected to house the six hundred visitors who came in canoes or on punts and bamboo rafts towed by the two mission launches. The old-timers wept with joy when they saw John and Susie. And when John and Susie were introduced to the second and third generations of the ones they knew so well, *they* wept with joy also. What a meeting that was! The years had taken nothing

from John's ability to preach in Fijian. And there was such
preaching and praising God that cannot be described.

On the Sabbath day there was an especially touching service
when Len V. Wilkinson, the principal of Mburesala, who had
endeared himself to all by his ministry to the young people, was
ordained. Then there followed a baptism for ten candidates.
There were others ready for this step, but for the sake of their
example the pastors requested that their baptism take place
back in their villages.

All too soon the *bose* was over, and the church members
departed and went slowly back to their homes.

For a few days the committee members remained to talk
over some of their problems. "One of our biggest problems just
now," said Roy Lane in introducing the subject, "is the future of
our training school. Brother Wilkinson, will you tell the
brethren what is on your mind?"

"Gladly," replied Len Wilkinson. "First of all, some of us
feel that we could strengthen our school and also our faculty if
we combined our girls' training school and our boys' training
school. The idea is a bit new and sounds a bit unworkable to
some of the government educators. But it has strengthened our
work in other countries, and I'm sure it would strengthen the
work here."

"I am sure it would also," added Arthur Dyason.

"I would even go one more step and combine the upper
grades of the Indian school with the Fijian training school," said
George Masters.

"And why not invite our neighbors from Tonga and Samoa
for the upper grades also?" added Gordon Branster.

"Now, Brother Fulton," said Andrew Stewart, "do you
think a coeducational multiracial college would work here in
Fiji?"

"Brethren, I *think* it would. I'm *sure* it would. It would

have its problems, of course," said John. Then he paused a
moment while a big genial smile lighted up his face. Then he
added, "I am also *sure* that I am glad that *I* was educated in a
coeducational school anyway." By the way everybody smiled it
was clear that the idea of a coeducational multiracial college
was what they all wanted for Fiji.

All too soon their visit in Fiji was over, and with their
hearts overflowing with joy, John and Susie proceeded to Australia. They arrived in Sydney, August 9, 1937, and what a
welcome awaited them there! John and Susie had served twenty-
three years in Australia, and everybody wanted to see them. It
was, of course, impossible to accept all of the invitations, but
John was glad to attend the Queensland and Northern Rivers
camp meetings in August, the union conference session in
September, and the South New South Wales camp meeting in
October.

Wherever he went he magnified the power of God and
gave the assurance that God is most certainly in this movement. He used to say, "When Mrs. Fulton and I came to the
Australian field forty years ago there were only 29,711 church
members in all the *world!* Today they tell me there are 28,479
Sabbath school members in the *Australian territory* alone!"

Finally the time came to say farewell to Australia for what
John and Susie both felt would be the last time on this old earth.
On Sabbath, November 6, he preached his final sermon in the
Wahroonga church. With his heart burdened with a desire to see
them all again, soon, in the kingdom of God, he chose for his
subject, "For the Time Is at Hand." He spoke briefly on the
prophecies that show Christ's coming is near. He reviewed
briefly the standards of the church that is preparing to meet
her Lord, and he closed with these words, "As I have traveled
here in Australia, again and again my heart has beat with joy
as I have come in contact with the saints of God, struggling on,

struggling upward, having that great goal before them as their only goal—readiness for the coming of Jesus. Oh, it is a solemn hour. God help us."

John and Susie were back in California for only about a year, when another unexpected invitation came to them. "Elder C. S. Prout in Hawaii is being transferred. How would you like to take his place as president of the Hawaiian Mission for a year or so?"

"Hawaii! Susie, how would you like that?" asked John.

"Oh, yes, John, I would love it. It would almost be like being back in Fiji again," replied Susie enthusiastically.

So from about the middle of 1939 to May, 1940, John and Susie were in lovely Hawaii, and as can be expected, they were greatly loved by everybody there.

Well, it was during this time they spent in Hawaii that a little farther over in the Pacific Ocean, in their own mission field of Fiji, one of the greatest rewards possible for a missionary was taking shape for John Fulton. The idea of the coeducational multiracial college for the Central Pacific Union Mission was definitely taking shape. In 1939 Len Wilkinson, who had been the principal of the Mburesala Training School, was made president of the Fiji Mission, and Arthur Dyason who had been on the faculty for six years was made principal of Mburesala. Already, after careful study, a site of four hundred acres near Korovou Tailevu on the main island of Viti Levu had been selected as the location for the new college.

Soon after being appointed president of the Fijian Mission, Pastor L. V. Wilkinson went on furlough, and Pastor Gordon Branster became acting president in his absence, so he called the committee together and said, "Brethren, we have a big job ahead of us. It is time for rebuilding our training school."

"And dismantling, transporting, and rebuilding some of the Samambula buildings," added George Masters.

16

"And also dismantling, transporting, and rebuilding of the Navuso girls' dormitory," added Eva Edwards.

"Yes, it's a huge job," said Gordon Branster. "Arthur, the responsibility will fall largely on you. Are you ready for it?"

"I am," replied Arthur with conviction. "And you will be interested to know that we have already talked it over at Mburesala, and it means that we can have no school at Mburesala this year. However, I am happy to tell you that forty of my big boys have agreed to work *without wages* for that year while they rebuild the school."

"That's the spirit!" said Gordon. "Arthur, we will all help." And they did. Building after building was carefully dismantled and the material carried to the beach and loaded onto barges. While this was being done, another band of boys cleared the land, making roads, and leveling the hilltops at the new location near Korovou, fifteen miles across the ocean.

When the barges were loaded they were towed one by one across the ocean by the mission launch to the new location. Sometimes the crossing was made in good weather and the trip was uneventful. But sometimes storms came up and made the crossing perilous. On one occasion, just after they had started one trip, a sudden strong wind blew up great waves on the ocean. As the storm increased, the waves became bigger and bigger. It was no use turning back. They were more than halfway across. They *had* to keep going. Suddenly one huge wave tipped the barge over so far that the ropes snapped. Some of the lumber fell into the ocean and the barge almost filled with water.

"Over the side, boys!" shouted Arthur Dyason. "Try to save the lumber!"

Quickly the boys jumped into the water. Some of them caught the floating boards. Some caught the ends of the ropes that had snapped. Fortunately there was a sand bar not too far away. The barge was pulled into the shallow water where the

Left:
Samoan students
at Fulton
Missionary College.

Below:
Tongan students
at Fulton
Missionary College.

Above:
Fijian girl students
at Fulton
Missionary College.

Right:
Indian girl students
at Fulton
Missionary College.

water could be pumped out of the barge and the lumber re-
loaded. By this time the worst of the storm was over and soon
they were on their way again.

Little by little the rebuilt buildings took shape. Soon the
boys' dormitory was finished, and the boys moved in. Then the
teachers' homes were finished and the teachers moved in. Last
of all the girls' dormitory was finished and the girls moved
in, and everybody was ready when it was time to open school
in 1941. There were 192 students!

"Now we need an official name for our new college," said
Gordon Branster as they met in committee.

"I have thought of one," said Arthur.

"I have too," said George.

"So have I," said Eva.

"Well, we will write the suggested names down and then
vote on them," said Gordon. "What name have you thought of,
Arthur?"

"Fulton College, after our great pioneer missionary to Fiji,"
he answered.

"Why, that's the same name I thought of," said George.

"And I also thought of that same name," added Eva. "Isn't
it strange?"

"No, it isn't strange," replied Gordon. "This school is certainly one of John Fulton's footprints. All in favor of naming
our training school 'Fulton College,' say, Aye."

And the ayes were unanimous. "Our college is destined to
become a great college," said Gordon Branster with conviction,
"for it is named after a great man." *

---

* These rebuilt buildings served for twenty-one more years. Then in 1962 and 1963
the administrative buildings and the dining room and kitchen were replaced with beautiful
modern steel-and-concrete-block buildings. Part of the funds for the rebuilding program
were provided by the Thirteenth Sabbath Offering overflow for the first quarter of 1963.
From an enrollment of 192 in 1941, the attendance at the college by 1967 had
grown to 442.
The academy and college students came from Tonga, Samoa, New Hebrides, Tahiti,
Cook, Pitcairn, Gilbert and Ellis, as well as from the many Fijian islands. Fulton College
did indeed become a great coeducational, multiracial college.

This happy news was telegraphed to John Fulton while he was in Hawaii. His eyes moistened and his chin quivered as he read it and passed it over to Susie. Then with a choked voice he said, "Oh, Susie, what an honor! What a reward! We don't deserve it. And to think we are still alive to enjoy the thrill of it. So many other colleges are named after men who are asleep in their graves."

John paused a moment, then added, "Susie, do you know what I wish?"

"I think I could guess pretty close to it," said Susie.

"I wish we were young again and could go to Fiji and do it all over again."

"So do I," breathed Susie.

After returning from Hawaii in 1940, John yearned for a quiet life on a little farm up in Oregon near to the place where he had spent his happy boyhood days. But it proved to be too far away from his daughters, Jessie and Agnes, who were living near Glendale, California, at the time, so he came down and lived in a pleasant little home in Sunland for about three years, 1941-1943. He was very happy there. He was asked to preach in the nearby churches every Sabbath as he was able. And Elder Glenn Calkins, the Pacific Union Conference president, who looked up to him as a son would look up to his father, frequently called on him for advice in the great administrative problems that confronted him. But by this time his years exceeded by four the three score years and ten that David speaks of, and his poor old tired heart began to give trouble. His normal pulse had always been a slow sixty, but now it frequently dropped to forty! Agnes felt anxious about him and begged Father and Mother Fulton to come and live in her home. So in 1944, they moved into an apartment in our house in Glendale.

Our home was near the sanitarium and the union conference headquarters, so he had many visitors—General Conference

Above:
Headquarters of the
Central Pacific Union Mission,
Tamavua, Viti Levu, 1951.
Agnes Fulton Hare
and Eric Howse are standing
in front of the building.

Right:
John E. Fulton
and his wife.

workers, overseas workers coming to and returning from meetings of one kind or another, and he treasured every visit.

One day in 1945 Elder Calkins dropped in, and said, "Daddy Fulton, I have some glad news for you today. You remember the new buildings we have been working on for La Sierra College ever since you were union conference president?"

"Of course I remember."

"Well, at last we have an appropriation for a new administration building and a new library building."

"I'm so glad," said John with a happy sigh. "We worked so hard to get them."

"And now, get ready for another thrill. Our committee has decided to call the library Fulton Memorial Library."

John reached over and took Elder Calkins' hand and squeezed it tight. He couldn't speak. Elder Calkins went on, "If all goes as planned, we start building next year, and in 1947 the library will be completed, and in 1947 we are going to have *you* come over and dedicate it!"

John's hand tightened again on Glenn's. "I'd love to," he breathed. "But it's too much honor. It's too great a reward. I have done so little to deserve it. Glenn, you must let someone else have that honor."

"Daddy Fulton," said Glenn tenderly, "that's just like you —so humble, always thinking of others. But I want you to know that we all feel that the reward is yours. You will never know how much the influence of your life and example have done for us younger workers."

They talked on for an hour or more, and when Elder Calkins left, John's face was radiant with joy.

The library at La Sierra College was completed in 1947 and named the Fulton Memorial Library, but John never knew it, and John didn't dedicate it, for he passed away April 23, 1945, at the age of seventy-six.

Above: Front view of Fulton Missionary College.

Below: Back view of Fulton Missionary College.

In April of 1945 Pastor E. B. Rudge was in Glendale on conference business, and on Sabbath, April 21, he came to visit John and Susie Fulton. At this time Pastor Rudge was the Australasian Union Conference president, but he had also been president of the Fiji Mission for eleven years, so they had a happy time together, talking over the success that had come to the various Fijian workers.

"And you'll be glad to know that Arthur Dyason is doing a wonderful job with Fulton College," said Pastor Rudge. "This year they have 263 students! Two hundred and forty-five in grades 1 to 8, and 18 in grades 9 to 12."

"And how many teachers?" asked John eagerly.

"Eleven," answered Pastor Rudge.

"I can remember when we had only one teacher!" said John. And he smiled a big smile of happy satisfaction.

"And there was a time," said Pastor Rudge, "when *you* were the only worker in Fiji. But you most certainly left your footprints everywhere you went, and although most of the old-timers of those days have passed away, their children and their grandchildren still speak your name affectionately. And now that our college bears your name, you will never be forgotten. Your deeds of valor will be passed on from one generation to another, and will continue to inspire and bless everyone in Fiji as long as time shall last."

They talked for an hour, and when Pastor Rudge left, Agnes said, "Thank you for coming, Brother Rudge. I haven't seen father so happy for many days."

That evening John had difficulty in going to sleep. Two weeks before, he had caught cold, and in spite of all they could do, it seemed impossible for him to throw it off. At midnight Agnes heard him stirring around, and going into his room, found him sitting up. He complained of shortness of breath. Agnes did what she could for him, and finally he did get some sleep. In the morning, however, she telephoned Dr. John Gregory, who was caring for him at the time, and told him about her father's restless night.

"Get him to the sanitarium by ambulance at once," the doctor directed. "I will meet him there."

The ambulance was called. John Fulton was taken to the hospital. Everything that love and medical skill could do was done for him, and his condition improved at once. His breathing became easier, he had a good sleep that night, and the next morning, Monday, April 23, he telephoned Agnes and said, "I am so much better. I am feeling fine. I even took my own sponge bath this morning."

During that morning Susie, Jessie, and Agnes called in at different times for brief visits. And he did seem much better. However, late that afternoon the nurse called on the telephone, "We notice a slight change in Elder Fulton's condition. You had better come up and stay close by."

They went up. One at a time they stood by his bed. He knew them. He spoke to them. "I'm just a little tired," he said.

Toward evening he was a little more tired. About six-thirty Susie stroked his forehead, and said, "Good night, John."

He replied, "*Good-by*, Susie dear."

Jessie stepped in to say good night, and to her also he said, "*Good-by*, Jessie dear."

To Agnes also he said, "*Good-by, Agnes dear.*"

Elders Calkins and D. A. Delafield were standing in the hall. Agnes went up to them and said, "It is strange, but instead of father saying 'good night,' as he usually does, he said '*good-by*.' Do you think maybe he has a premonition that his end is near?"

The two ministers went in and had a short word of prayer with him. "Thank you," he said, and gently squeezed their hands.

About seven-thirty Dr. Gregory went in. John brightened

up when he heard his voice, and as the doctor left he said, "Good-night, Doctor. I'll see you in the morning."

Those were the last words he spoke. About eight o'clock the nurse opened the door, and beckoned the doctor to come in. And in a few miments he came out again and said softly, "He's gone."

On Sabbath afternoon April 28, 1945, John Fulton was laid to rest in the Grand View Memorial park, by Elder Calkins, Elder Rudge, and Elder Delafield, to wait till Jesus comes.

Susie Fulton lived on for five more years, till at the age of seventy-nine she fell asleep on March 30, 1950. She was buried by the side of her valiant lifelong companion.

So, though the great Fiji pioneer John Edwin Fulton sleeps, the influence of his life and example, the influence of his footprints in Fiji, will live on as long as time shall last, and then, to use his own last words, we, if faithful, shall see him "in the morning."

BIBLIOGRAPHY

Christensen, Alta H. *In Strange Peril on Dark Trails*. Washington, D.C.: Review and Herald Publishing Association, © 1958.

Gates, E. H. *In Coral Isles*. Washington, D.C.: Review and Herald Publishing Association, © 1923.

Glover, R. H. *The Progress of World-wide Missions*. New York: Harper, © 1960.

Leonard, D. L. *A Hundred Years of Missions*. New York: Funk and Wagnalls Company, © 1895, 1903.

Mason, A. DeW. *Outlines of Missionary History*. New York: Hodder and Stoughton, © 1912, 1916.

National Geographic Magazine. October, 1958.

Pierson, A. T. *The Modern Mission Century Viewed as a Cycle of Divine Working*. New York: The Baker and Taylor Company, © 1901.

Seventh-day Adventist Encyclopedia. Washington, D.C.: Review and Herald Publishing Association, © 1966.

Spalding, A. W. *Captains of the Host*. Washington, D.C.: Review and Herald Publishing Association, © 1949.

————, *Christ's Last Legion*. Washington, D.C.: Review and Herald Publishing Association, © 1949.

Spicer, W. A. *Our Story of Missions*. Mountain View, Calif.: Pacific Press Publishing Association, © 1921.

Stewart, A. G. *Trophies From Cannibal Isles*. Washington, D.C.: Review and Herald Publishing Association, © 1952.

Vernon, R. *James Calvert, or From Dark to Dawn in Fiji*. London: S. W. Partridge & Co., 1890.

Watson, C. H. *Adventures in the South Seas*. Washington, D.C.: Review and Herald Publishing Association, © 1931.